THE **TESTING** SERIES

PARAMEDIC
TESTS

THE **TESTING** SERIES
expert advice on interview preparation

 how2become

Orders: Please contact How2become Ltd, Suite 2,
50 Churchill Square Business Centre, Kings Hill, Kent ME19 4YU.

Telephone: (44) 0845 643 1299 - Lines are open Monday to Friday 9am until 5pm.
You can also order via the email address info@how2become.co.uk.

ISBN: 9781907558139

First published 2011

Typeset for How2become Ltd by Molly Hill, Canada.

Printed in Great Britain for How2become Ltd by: CMP (uk) Limited, Poole, Dorset.

CONTENTS

PREFACE
BY AUTHOR
RICHARD MCMUNN

During my time in the Fire Service I had the chance to meet and work with many paramedics and emergency care assistants (ECA's). Every single one of them was a true professional and they always took tremendous pride in their work. I attended many road traffic collisions, house fires and rail accidents in my time, and more often than not I was required to work alongside these brave men and women. Not once did they fail in their duty to provide a high level of care to those people who needed them most.

Whilst in the Fire Service I also managed to speak to many different people who were directly involved in the recruitment process for joining the Ambulance Service, and I was also fortunate enough to enjoy a day riding with an ambulance crew attending many different operational incidents. Having asked a number of them what it takes to pass the selection process, one word kept constantly coming up – preparation!

I have always been a great believer in preparation. Preparation was my key to success, and it is also yours. Without the right level of preparation you will be setting out on the route to failure. The Ambulance Service is very hard to join, but if you follow the steps that I have compiled within this guide then you will increase your chances of success dramatically.

Remember, you are learning how to be a successful candidate, not a successful paramedic.

Before you apply to join the Ambulance Service, you need to be fully confident that you too are capable of providing a high level of service. If you think you can do it, and you can rise to the challenge, then you just might be the type of person the Ambulance Service is looking for.

As with any guide that I write, or training course that I run, I always focus the student's mind on the qualities that are required to carry out a specific job competently. More often than not recruiters will assess you against these qualities during the selection process and therefore you must concentrate your preparation on this area.

Enjoy the tests!

Best wishes,

Richard McMunn
Managing Director and Founder
How2Become.co.uk

CHAPTER 1
ABOUT THE PARAMEDICS TESTS

During the paramedic selection process you will be required to undertake a number of psychometric tests. Whilst the type of tests will vary from trust to trust, the most common forms of assessment include:

- Numerical reasoning test;
- Verbal reasoning test;
- Highway Code test.

The reason why the trust will use the above tests to assess potential student paramedics is simply because they provide an accurate appraisal of how a person might perform in the role. As you can imagine, paramedics need to be competent in the use of numbers whilst administering drugs to a patient and carrying out general patient treatment. They have to be competent in the use of the written word because they will be writing important notes that relate to their treatment of a patient. The memory test is used because, as a paramedic, you will have to retain a large amount of job relevant information and recall it during highly pressurised incidents. Finally, the Highway Code is used as an assessment simply because you will be driving an Ambulance under 999 conditions.

Within this guide I have provided you with a large number of tips and practice test questions covering each area. It is important to note that the following tests are provided as a practice aid only and they should not be relied upon to be an accurate reflection of the real tests.

HOW TO PREPARE FOR THE PARAMEDIC TESTS

It is crucial that you set aside plenty of time to prepare for the tests. Only you will know what areas you are competent in and what areas you need to improve on. Whilst preparing for the tests you should aim for speed and accuracy. The more sample test questions you try, the faster and more accurate you will become. It is far better to practice a small number of tests every night in the build up to the tests rather than 'cramming' the night before. As soon as you have submitted your application form for becoming a paramedic you should start preparing for the tests and interview straight away.

Most applicants will wait until they hear whether or not their application form has been successful before sitting down and preparing for the tests; however, this is losing them valuable preparation time. You need to start your preparation immediately!

The results of the tests are used as part of the entire selection process and not in isolation. Just because a candidate achieves a lower than average score on the numerical tests, this does not automatically mean they can't become a highly competent paramedic. However, a very poor score might be a cause for concern for the recruiter. You should be aiming for high scores in every element of the selection process and that also includes the written tests.

Prior to the tests

> Preparation, preparation, preparation! In the weeks before the test, work hard to improve your skills in the testing areas. In addition to the tests contained within this guide there are numerous other testing resources available at www.how2become.co.uk. Practice as many test questions as possible and make sure you learn from your mistakes!

> Get a good night's sleep before the test day and don't drink any alcohol or caffeine.

> On the morning of the test get up early and have a last practice at a small number of sample test questions just to get your brain working.

> Eat a good healthy breakfast such as bran flakes and a chopped up banana. Don't eat anything too heavy that will make you feel bloated or sluggish – remember; you want to be at your best! Drink plenty of water too.

> Check the news for any potential traffic problems and leave in good time to arrive at the test centre with plenty of time to spare. Take a small bottle of water with you to help keep you hydrated.

On The Day

> Arrive in good time at the test location. Make sure you know where the test centre is.

> Ensure that you know exactly what you are required to do - do not be afraid to ask questions.

> Follow the instructions you are given exactly.

> During the tests try to eliminate as many wrong answers as possible. For example, with numerical tests and verbal reasoning tests, a quick estimate may help you to discard several of the options without working out every alternative.

> Work as quickly and accurately as you can. Both speed and accuracy are important so do not spend too long on any one question.

> Do not waste time on a difficult question. If you are stuck, leave it and move on but make sure you leave a space on the answer sheet.

> Don't worry if you do not finish all the questions in the time, but if you do, go over your answers again to check them.

> Wear smart, formal dress. Remember that you are trying to create a good impression. You are attempting to join a uniformed service so it is advisable that you wear an appropriate outfit. Many people at the test centre will be wearing jeans and trainers. Make sure you stand out for all the right reasons.

> Keep your head down and concentrate on the task in hand. It is your job to do as best as you possibly can during the tests so it is important that you concentrate.

Now move on to the next section of the guide. You will notice that I have provided you with a large number of test questions to help you prepare. Work through the questions carefully sticking to the allocated time limits.

CHAPTER 2
NUMERICAL REASONING TESTS

Try to answer the questions quickly and without the use of a calculator. You have 5 minutes in which to answer the 14 questions.

Exercise 1

1. A wallet has been found containing one £20 note, five £5 notes, a fifty pence coin and three 2 pence coins. How much is in the wallet?

Answer

2. Subtract 200 from 500, add 80, subtract 30 and multiply by 2. What number do you have?

Answer

3. A multi-storey car park has 8 floors and can hold 72 cars on each floor. In addition to this there is also allocation for 4 disabled parking spaces per floor. How many spaces are there in the entire car park?

Answer

4. A man saves £12.50 per month. How much would he have saved after 1 year?

Answer [   ]

5. If there have been 60 accidents along one stretch of a motorway in the last year, how many on average have occurred each month?

Answer [   ]

6. Out of 40,000 paramedic applicants only 4,000 are likely to be successful. What percentage will fail?

Answer [   ]

7. What percentage of 400 is 100?

Answer [   ]

8. Malcolm's shift commences at 0615 hours. If his shift is 10.5 hours long what time will he finish?

Answer [   ]

9. If Mary can bake 12 cakes in 2 hours how many will she bake in 10 hours?

Answer [   ]

10. If there are 24 hours in the day. How many hours are there in one week?

Answer [   ]

11. Susan has 10 coins and gives 5 of them to Steven and the remainder to Alan. Alan gives 3 of his coins to Steven who in turn gives half of his back to Susan. How many is Susan left with?

Answer [   ]

12. Add 121 to 54. Now subtract 75 and multiply by 10. What is the result?

Answer [   ]

13. Ahmed leaves for work at 8am and arrives at work at 9.17am. He then leaves work at 4.57pm and arrives back at home at 6.03pm. How many minutes has Ahmed spent travelling?

Answer [   ]

14. A car travels at 30 km/h for the first hour, 65km/h for the second hour, 44 km/h for the third hour and 50 km/h for the fourth hour. What is the car's average speed over the 4-hour journey?

Answer [   ]

Now move on to exercise 2.

Exercise 2

You are not permitted to use a calculator during this exercise. You have 10 minutes in which to answer 20 multiple-choice questions

1. Your friends tell you their electricity bill has gone up from £40 per month to £47 per month. How much extra are they now paying per year?

a. £84   b. £85   c. £83   d. £86   e. £82

Answer [ ]

2. A woman earns a salary of £32,000 per year. How much would she earn in 15 years?

a. £280,000   b. £380,000   c. £480,000   d. £260,000   e. £460,000

Answer [ ]

3. If a police officer walks the beat for 6 hours at a pace of 4km/h, how much ground will she have covered after the 6 hours is over?

a. 20km   b. 21km   c. 22km   d. 23km   e. 24km

Answer [ ]

4. It takes Malcolm 45 minutes to walk 6 miles to work. At what pace does he walk?

a. 7 mph   b. 4 mph   c. 6 mph   d. 5 mph   e. 8 mph

Answer [ ]

5. Ellie spends 3 hours on the phone talking to her friend abroad. If the call costs 12 pence per 5 minutes, how much does the call cost in total?

a. £3.30   b. £4.32   c. £3.32   d. £4.44   e. £3.44

Answer [ ]

6. A woman spends £27 in a retail store. She has a discount voucher that reduces the total cost to £21.60. How much discount does the voucher give her?

a. 5%   b. 10%   c. 15%   d. 20%   e. 25%

Answer

7. A group of 7 men spend £21.70 on a round of drinks. How much does each of them pay if the bill is split evenly?

a. £3.00   b. £65.10   c. £3.10   d. £3.15   e. £3.20

Answer

8. 45,600 people attend a football match to watch Manchester United play Tottenham Hotspur. If there are 32,705 Manchester United supporters at the game, how many Tottenham Hotspur supporters are there?

a. 12,985   b. 13,985   c. 12, 895   d. 12,895   e. 14, 985

Answer

9. The Ambulance Service are called to attend a motorway accident involving a coach full of passengers. A total of 54 people are on board, 17 of whom are injured. How many are not injured?

a. 40   b. 39   c. 38   d. 37   e. 36

Answer

10. A car journey usually takes 6 hrs and 55 minutes, but on one occasion the car stops for a total of 47 minutes. How long does the journey take on this occasion?

a. 6 hrs 40 mins
b. 5 hrs 45 mins
c. 7 hrs 40 mins
d. 7 hrs 42 mins
e. 6 hrs 42 mins

Answer

11. There are 10 people in a team. Five of them weigh 70 kg each and the remaining 5 weigh 75 kg each. What is the average weight of the team?

a. 72.5 kg   b. 71.5 kg   c. 70.5 kg   d. 72 kg   e. 71 kg

Answer

12. A kitchen floor takes 80 tiles to cover. A man buys 10 boxes, each containing 6 tiles. How many more boxes does he need to complete the job?

a. 2 boxes   b. 4 boxes   c. 6 boxes   d. 8 boxes   e. 10 boxes

Answer

13. How much money does it cost to buy 12 packets of crisps at 47 pence each?

a. £6.45   b. £5.64   c. £6.54   d. £4.65   e. £5.46

Answer

14. A motorcyclist is travelling at 78 mph on a road where the speed limit is 50 mph. How much over the speed limit is he?

a. 20 mph   b. 22 mph   c. 26 mph   d. 28 mph   e. 30 mph

Answer

15. A removal firm loads 34 boxes onto a van. If there are 27 boxes still to be loaded, how many boxes are there in total?

a. 49   b. 50   c. 61   d. 52   e. 53

Answer

16. When paying a bill at the bank you give the cashier one £20 note, two £5 notes, four £1 coins, six 10p coins and two 2p coins. How much have you given him?

 THE **TESTING** SERIES

A. £34.64   b. £43.46   C. £34.46   d. £63.44   e. £36.46

Answer [　　]

17. If you pay £97.70 per month on your council tax bill, how much would you pay quarterly?

a. £293.30   b. £293.20   c. £293.10   d. £293.00   e. £292.90

Answer [　　]

18. Four people eat a meal at a restaurant. The total bill comes to £44.80. How much do they need to pay each?

a. £10.00   b. £10.10   c. £10.20   d. £11.10   e. £11.20

Answer [　　]

19. A worker is required to work for 8 hours a day. He is entitled to three 20-minute breaks and one 1-hour lunch break during that 8-hour period. If he works for 5 days per week, how many hours will he have worked after 4 weeks?

a. 12 hours   b. 14 hours   c. 120 hours   d. 140 hours   e. 150 hours

Answer [　　]

20. If there are 610 metres in a mile, how many metres are there in 4 miles?

a. 240   b. 2040   c. 2044   d. 2440   e. 244

Answer [　　]

ANSWERS TO NUMERICAL REASONING EXERCISE 1

1. £45.56

2. 700

3. 608

4. £150

5. 5

6. 90%

7. 25%

8. 1645 hours or 4.45pm

9. 60 cakes

10. 168

11. 4

12. 1000

13. 143 minutes

14. 47.25 km/h

ANSWERS TO NUMERICAL REASONING EXERCISE 2

1. a. £84
In this question you need to first work out the difference in their electricity bill. Subtract £40 from £47 to be left with £7. Now you need to calculate how much extra they are paying per year. If there are 12 months in a year then you need to multiply £7 by 12 months to reach your answer of £84.

2. c. £480,000
The lady earns £32,000 per year. To work out how much she earns in 15 years, you must multiply £32,000 by 15 years to reach your answer of £480,000.

3. e. 24km
To work this answer out all you need to do is multiply the 6 hours by the 4 km/h to reach the total of 24 km. Remember that she is walking at a pace of 4 km per hour for a total of 6 hours.

 THE **TESTING** SERIES

4. e. 8mph

Malcolm walks 6 miles in 45 minutes, which means he is walking two miles every 15 minutes. Therefore, he would walk 8 miles in 60 minutes (1 hour), so he is walking at 8 mph.

5. b. £4.32

If the call costs 12 pence for every 5 minutes then all you need to do is calculate how many 5 minutes there are in the 3-hour telephone call. There are 60 minutes in every hour, so therefore there are 180 minutes in 3 hours. 180 minutes divided by 5 minutes will give you 36. To get your answer, just multiply 36 by 12 pence to reach your answer of £4.32

6. d. 20%

This type of question can be tricky, especially when you don't have a calculator! The best way to work out the answer is to first of all work out how much 10% discount would give you off the total price. If £27 is the total price, then 10% would be a £2.70 discount. In monetary terms the woman has received £5.40 in discount. If 10% is a £2.70 discount then 20% is a £5.40 discount.

7. c. £3.10

Divide £21.70 by 7 to reach your answer of £3.10.

8. d. 12,895

Subtract 32,705 from 45,600 to reach your answer of 12,895.

9. d. 37

Subtract 17 from 54 to reach your answer of 37.

10. d. 7 hrs 42 minutes

Add the 47 minutes to the normal journey time of 6 hrs and 55 minutes to reach your answer of 7 hrs and 42 minutes.

11. a. 72.5 kg

To calculate the average weight, you need to first of all add each weight together. Therefore, (5 x 70) + (5 x 75) = 725 kg. To find the average weight you must now divide the 725 by 10, which will give you the answer 72.5 kg.

12. b. 4 boxes

The man has 10 boxes, each of which contains 6 tiles. He therefore has a total of 60 tiles. He now needs a further 20 tiles to cover the total floor area. If there are 6 tiles in a box then he will need a further 4 boxes (24 tiles).

13. b. £5.64
Multiply 12 by 47 pence to reach your answer of £5.64.

14. d. 28 mph
Subtract 50 mph from 78 mph to reach your answer of 28 mph.

15. c. 61
Add 34 to 27 to reach your answer of 61 boxes.

16. a. £34.64
Add all of the currency together to reach the answer of £34.64.

17. c. £293.10
To reach the answer you must multiply £97.70 by 3. Remember, a quarter is every 3 months.

18. e. £11.20
Divide £44.80 by 4 people to reach your answer of £11.20.

19. c. 120 hours
First of all you need to determine how many 'real' hours he works each day. Subtract the total sum of breaks from 8 hours to reach 6 hours per day. If he works 5 days per week then he is working a total of 30 hours per week. Multiply 30 hours by 4 weeks to reach your answer of 120 hours.

20. d. 2440 metres
Multiply 4 by 610 metres to reach your answer of 2440 metres.

Now move on to Numerical Reasoning Tests part two.

PART 2

You have 12 minutes to complete 25 questions. Please circle the correct answer. You are not permitted to use a calculator at any point in the test.

Practice Test 1

1. A garage is selling three used cars. The mileage on the first is 139,500, the mileage on the second is 120,500, and the mileage on the third is 160,000. What is the average mileage of the three used cars?

a. 140,000
b. 145,000
c. 150,000
d. 135,000
e. 130,000

2. You are called to an accident 120 miles away. It takes you 1 hour 30 minutes to arrive at the accident site. What speed have you been driving at?

a. 80 mph
b. 60 mph
c. 40 mph
d. 50 mph
e. 45 mph

3. You decide to walk the 10 miles home following your shift. It takes you 2 hours. What speed do you walk at in miles per hour?

a. 60 mph
b. 20 mph
c. 10 mph
d. 5 mph
e. 15 mph

4. During the transportation of a patient you average 30 mph over 1 hour 20 minutes. What distance have you covered in this time?

a. 32 miles
b. 40 miles
c. 50 miles
d. 43 miles
e. 45 miles

5. Sam, Steve and Mark are brothers. Sam is 36, Steve is 28 and Mark is 26. What is their average age?

a. 29
b. 32
c. 31
d. 33
e. 30

6. There are four suspects in a police line-up. Suspect A is 1.20m tall, suspect B is 1.25m tall, suspect C is 1.55m tall and suspect D is 1.6m tall. What is the average height of the suspects?

a. 1.41m
b. 1.40m
c. 1.42m
d. 1.39m
e. 1.37m

7. The perimeter of the Ambulance Station yard is 240 metres. The yard has a square perimeter. What is the average length of a side of the yard?

a. 40 metres
b. 50 metres
c. 60 metres
d. 120 metres
e. 130 metres

8. The police are escorting approximately 540 football fans to the train station. A train can carry 135 people. How many trains will be needed to transport the fans?

a. 2 to 3
b. 4 to 5
c. 6 to 7
d. 8 to 9
e. 9 to 10

9. Darren commutes to and from work every day from Monday to Friday. His office is 40 miles away from his house. How many miles does Darren drive per week?

a. 200
b. 400

c. 800

d. 1,000

e. 1,200

10. John runs a marathon (26 miles) with 69 other runners. Every single runner completes the marathon. What is the combined distance run by all the runners?

a. 1784

b. 1830

c. 1794

d. 1820

e. 1824

11. You bicycle for 2 hours at an average speed of 18 mph. What distance have you travelled in total?

a. 9 miles

b. 20 miles

c. 36 miles

d. 24 miles

e. 22 miles

12. John is a tree surgeon who is paid to cut down a dead oak tree. The tree is 90 metres tall. John has to cut the tree into 4.5m sections. How many cuts will he have to make?

a. 10

b. 45

c. 30

d. 40

e. 20

13. You own a market stall and sell 216 apples. You have sold apples to 36 customers. On average how many apples did each customer buy?

a. 4

b. 6

c. 8

d. 12

e. 14

14. The Metropolitan Police have 1,200 police officers on duty. They want 300 areas patrolled. How many police officers should go on each patrol?

a. 2

b. 3

c. 5

d. 6

e. 4

15. A leisure complex has three pools: pool A, pool B and pool C. What is the area of swimming pool A?

a. 6 m²

b. 10 m²

c. 12 m²

d. 14 m²

e. 21 m²

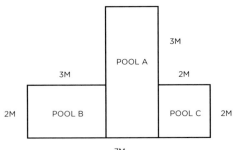

16. What is the average weekly wage of a team of five people whose individual wages are: £59.00, £61.00, £64.00, £76.00 and £80.00?

a. £64

b. £68

c. £73

d. £76

e. £77

17. Response times to emergency calls vary throughout the week; on Monday it is 7 minutes, on Tuesday it's 7 minutes, on Wednesday it's 5 minutes, on Thursday it's 6 minutes, on Friday it's 9 minutes, on Saturday it's 8 minutes and finally on Sunday it's 7 minutes. What is the average response time?

a. 6 minutes

b. 5 minutes

c. 8 minutes

d. 9 minutes

e. 7 minutes

18. There are 7 new paramedics at a Wolverhampton Ambulance Station. Their ages are 18, 19, 21, 24, 28, 29 and 36. What is their average age?

a. 22 years old
b. 24 years old
c. 25 years old
d. 26 years old
e. 27 years old

19. There are 150 guests at a Spanish holiday complex. 50 of the guests are British, 35 are German, 10 are French, and 5 are Italian. The rest of the guests are Spanish. What percentage of guests are Spanish?

a. 33.33%
b. 32%
c. 33%
d. 66.66%
e. 70%

20. Using the chart below, on average how many people would use the bus over a 4-month period?

a. 40
b. 45
c. 60
d. 80
e. 90

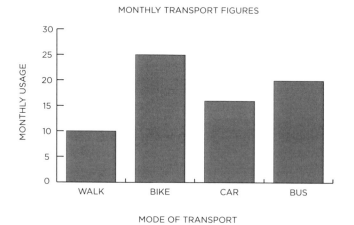

MONTHLY TRANSPORT FIGURES

MONTHLY USAGE

MODE OF TRANSPORT

WALK BIKE CAR BUS

21. Using the chart above, calculate the combined total of people who walk and use a bike as a mode of transport per month?

a. 25
b. 30
c. 35
d. 40
e. 45

22. The Ambulance Service receive 1,200 applications for every 60 available posts. What is this as a fraction?

a. 4/1
b. 20/1
c. 30/1
d. 40/1
e. 45/1

23. A container ship carries 1,000 barrels. Each barrel contains 330 litres of oil. How much oil is contained in the barrels?

a. 330 litres
b. 3,300 litres
c. 33,000 litres
d. 330,000 litres
e. 3,300,000 litres

24. A bike company has 12 factories each producing 102 bikes a day. How many bikes does the company produce per day?

a. 1,004
b. 1,040
c. 1,204
d. 1,224
e. 1,226

25. A carpet factory operates 24 hours a day. If the factory produces 10 carpets an hour, how many carpets are produced in a day?

a. 220
b. 240
c. 260
d. 280
e. 290

Now move on to practice test 2.

 THE **TESTING** SERIES

Practice Test 2

You have 12 minutes to complete 25 questions. Please circle the correct answer. You are not permitted to use a calculator at any point in the test.

1. In a biscuit tin there are 28 biscuits. If you were to divide these equally between a family of 4, how many biscuits would each family member get?

a. 7
b. 4
c. 8
d. 3.5
e. 5

2. A plane can carry 180 passengers. There are 36 rows on the plane. How many passengers are there on each row?

a. 9
b. 6
c. 7
d. 8
e. 5

3. You have been driving in your Ambulance for 2 hours 15 minutes at a constant speed of 48 mph. How far have you driven so far?

a.   180 miles
b.   108 miles
c.   104 miles
d.   140 miles
e.   144 miles

4. A sprinter runs 200 metres in 22 seconds. How long would it take him to run 2,000 metres if he continued to run at the same speed?

a. 3 minutes 40 seconds
b. 3 minutes 20 seconds
c. 4 minutes 20 seconds
d. 3 minutes 15 seconds
e. 4 minutes 15 seconds

5. Samantha is a carpenter. She makes 3 oak tables for a family. The first table top measures 0.75 x 2 metres, the second measures 1.5 x 3 metres and the third measures 1.0 x 3 metres. What is the average area of the table tops?

a. 5 m²
b. 4 m²
c. 3 m²
d. 2 m²
e. 2.5 m²

6. Five students buy a pizza each. Each pizza costs £5.20. The students are each given 10% discount. What is the total bill for the students?

a. £23.20
b. £23.40
c. £23.60
d. £24.40
e. £24.60

7. At a campsite there are 240 tents. During a flood, 2.5% of the tents are damaged. How many tents were damaged during the flood?

a. 6
b. 8
c. 5
d. 9
e. 4

8. In your savings account there is £13,000. You decide to withdraw 40% to buy a car. How much money do you withdraw?

a. £520
b. £5,200
c. £7,200
d. £8,000
e. £8,200

9. You own a Ford Fiesta which is currently worth £8000. Since you bought the car it has depreciated in value by 30% of its original value. How much was the original value of the vehicle?

a. £8,240
b. £11,400
c. £10,400
d. £12,400
e. £12,450

10. A ticket for a football match costs £12. If 12,000 people go to the game, how much in total will ticket sales make?

a. £14,400
b. £144,000
c. £288,000
d. £144,0000
e. £420,000

11. A solicitor charges £28 per hour for legal services. If you hired a solicitor for 12 hours, how much would you be charged?

a. £326
b. £336
c. £374
d. £436
e. £442

12. At Uxbridge Grammar there are 200 students. 15 of the students get straight A's. What is this as a percentage?

a. 7.5%
b. 10%
c. 15%
d. 30%
e. 45%

13. You find a missing wallet in the street. It contains a £10 note, two £5 notes, three £1 coins, a 50p coin and six 2p coins. How much is in the wallet?

a. £22.72
b. £22.62
c. £24.62
d. £23.56
e. £23.62

14. Your car does 35 miles to the gallon. The car takes 8 gallons of petrol full. If you were to drive 560 miles how much petrol would you need?

a. 12 gallon
b. 14 gallons
c. 16 gallons
d. 18 gallons
e. 24 gallons

15. Two farmers, Jack and Tom, both own adjoining fields. What is the total combined area of both Jack's and Tom's fields?

a. 160m2
b. 240m2
c. 800m2
d. 1600m2
e. 2400m2

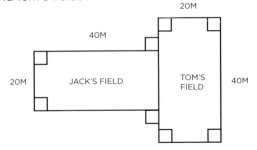

16. On average a bank repossesses 3 out of 150 homes every year. The village of Claxby has 1,000 homes. Under the above principle, how many homes would be repossessed in the village?

a. 10
b. 15
c. 20
d. 25
e. 30

17. A school has 15 classes with 23 students in each class. How many students are at the school?

a. 245
b. 325
c. 335
d. 445
e. 345

18. A restaurant serves 60 customers a night. If on average each customer spends £30, what is the total average for the night?

a. £180
b. £1,600
c. £2,400
d. £1,800
e. £1,260

19. A chocolate bar costs 59p. If you were to buy 6 chocolate bars, how much would it cost you?

a. £3.34
b. £3.45
c. £3.54
d. £4.24
e. £4.14

20. You fly a three-leg journey in a light aircraft. The total distance covered is 270 miles. What is the average distance of each leg?

a. 70 miles
b. 80 miles
c. 90 miles
d. 135 miles
e. 140 miles

21. A team of 12 explorers find the wreck of a ship. The ship contains 6 gold bars each worth £120,000. How much money does each team member make?

a. £40,000
b. £60,000
c. £100,000
d. £120,000
e. £130,000

22. Below is a pie-chart representing crime in the town of Upton. Based on an estimated 100 crimes, use the pie-chart below to estimate the number of burglary-related crimes.

a. 17
b. 20
c. 27
d. 34
e. 170

DAILY CRIME FIGURES - UPTON

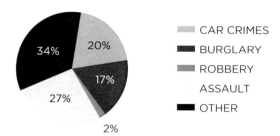

23. A magazine on average contains 110 pages. If you bought seven magazines, how many pages are there in total?

a. 700

b. 720

c. 740

d. 770

e. 780

24. A car is travelling at 72 miles per hour. How many miles will it have travelled in 45 minutes?

a. 54

b. 52

c. 50

d. 48

e. 46

25. If carpet costs 1.20 per metre, how much will 35 metres of carpet cost?

a. £45.00

b. £43.75

c. £44.00

d. £46.75

e. £42.00

Now move on to practice test 3.

Practice Test 3

You have 12 minutes to complete 25 questions. Please circle the correct answer. You are not permitted to use a calculator at any point in the test.

1. If 70% of £500 has been spent, how much money remains?

a. £125
b. £130
c. £140
d. £150
e. £160

2. A multi-storey office has 7 floors, and each floor has 49 employees. How many members of staff work in the multi-storey office?

a. 257
b. 343
c. 357
d. 423
e. 475

3. Following some road works on the M1 the highways agency need their 5 vehicles to collect 1,250 cones. On average how many cones do each of the 5 vehicles have to collect?

a. 125
b. 200
c. 250
d. 500
e. 525

4. Laura buys three items: a pair of shoes, a dress, and a coat. The items totalled £340. If the shoes were £59.99 and the coat was £139.99, how much was the dress?

a. £138.02
b. £138.00
c. £140.02
d. £142.00
e. £144.00

5. At Telford school there are 200 school students. 25 students get straight A's. What is this as a percentage?

a. 12.5%
b. 10%
c. 15%
d. 30%
e. 25%

6. A carton of milk costs £1.19. How much change would you have left from £5.00 if you bought one carton?

a. £2.81
b. £3.61
c. £3.71
d. £3.81
e. £4.05

7. You are driving down a motorway at 108 mph. How far do you travel in 25 minutes?

a. 47 miles
b. 45 miles
c. 44 miles
d. 42 miles
e. 41 miles

8. A fast jet is flying at a speed of 270 mph. The distance from airfield A to airfield B is 90 miles. How long does it take to fly from A to B?

a. 20 minutes
b. 24 minutes
c. 22 minutes
d. 26 minutes
e. 28 minutes

9. You are travelling down a motorway. Your journey has lasted 50 minutes and you have covered 125 miles. What speed have you been travelling at?

a. 162 mph
b. 155 mph
c. 160 mph
d. 152 mph
e. 150 mph

10. If the Ambulance Service on average responds to 25 emergency calls a day, how many do they respond to in a week?

a. 160
b. 165
c. 170
d. 175
e. 180

11. Lincolnshire, Yorkshire and Lancashire all have new police helicopters. It takes the Lincolnshire helicopter 15 minutes to fly to Leeds, the Lancashire helicopter takes 35 minutes and the Yorkshire helicopter takes 10 minutes. What is the average time it takes these three helicopters to get to Leeds?

a. 15 minutes
b. 20 minutes
c. 25 minutes
d. 30 minutes
e. 35 minutes

12. A car park has 500 available spaces. On a busy day 75% of these are full. How many full car parking spaces are there on a busy day?

a. 375
b. 350
c. 325
d. 320
e. 310

13. You have £50 in your wallet and spend 70% of it on shopping. How much money have you spent on shopping?

a. £30
b. £35
c. £40
d. £50
e. £45

14. The Metropolitan police force has 120,000 officers. 3% of these officers are due to retire. How many officers will retire?

a. 360,000
b. 36,000
c. 360
d. 36
e. 3,600

15. The road tax for your car cost £120 in 2007. In 2008 it increases by 10%. How much is the road tax in 2008?

a. £121.20
b. £132
c. £142
d. £152
e. £152.20

16. A school decides to buy 12 laptops costing £850 each. What is the combined cost for the 12 laptops?

a. £10,200
b. £10,400
c. £10,500
d. £10,600
e. £10,800

17. A metre of wool costs 62p. How much would it cost to buy 6 metres of wool?

a. £3.72
b. £3.62
c. £3.82
d. £4.72
e. £5.12

18. Sally is riding her horse in a cross country competition. She has been told that she has to complete the course in 2 hours and 30 minutes. If divided into equal quarters, how long should she aim to spend completing each phase?

a. 35 minutes
b. 37.5 minutes
c. 35.5 minutes
d. 38.5 minutes
e. 39.5 minutes

19. There are 18 teams entered in a rugby competition. If there are 6 changing rooms, how many teams use each changing room?

a. 2
b. 4
c. 6
d. 3
e. 5

20. Using the diagram below, calculate the perimeter of the inner rectangle?

a. 16.4 cm
b. 17.2 cm
c. 17.8 cm
d. 18.4 cm
e. 18.8 cm

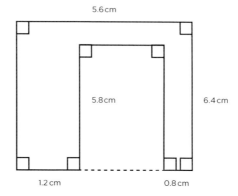

21. A room measures 20m by 5m. If I wanted to carpet 50% of it and I had 60 square metres of carpet available, how many square metres would I have left after finishing the task?

a. 5m²
b. 10m²
c. 15m²
d. 20m²
e. 25m²

22. If a ferry journey of 490 miles takes 7 hours, what is the average speed of the ferry?

a. 55 mph
b. 60 mph
c. 65 mph
d. 70 mph
e. 80 mph

23. A multi-storey car park has 8 levels. Each level has 111 car parking spaces. How many cars will be in the car park when it is full?

a. 784
b. 888
c. 988
d. 8,888
e. 9,988

24. The Ambulance Service Training Centre sweepstake wins £1,500. If this is divided by 25 employees, how much does each employee win?

a. £30
b. £40
c. £60
d. £80
e. £85

25. Below is a line graph showing car sales for Manby Autos from January to April. Calculate the total combined car sales for February and March.

a. 900
b. 8,000
c. 9,000
d. 10,000
e. 12,000

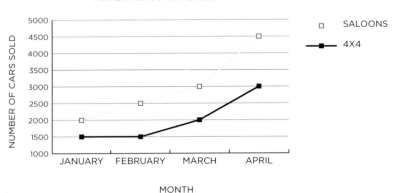

MANBY AUTOS CAR SALES

Now move on to practice test 4.

Practice Test 4

You have 12 minutes to complete 25 questions. Please circle the correct answer. You are not permitted to use a calculator at any point in the test.

1. A yearly golf subscription costs £150 in 2007. It is expected to rise by 15% in 2008. How much will the yearly subscription cost in 2008?

a. £172.50
b. £172.20
c. £172
d. £165.72
e. £162.50

2. In a cross country competition there are 138 runners, 23 runners do not finish the race. What is this as a fraction?

a. 1/5
b. 1/6
c. 1/8
d. 1/12
e. 1/4

3. A football pitch is approximately 110 metres long. If you had 11 football pitches, one after the other, how long would the total distance be?

a. 1,110 metres
b. 1,420 metres
c. 1,390 metres
d. 1,440 metres
e. 1,210 metres

4. One out of twelve people in a group of football fans support Manchester United. If there are 2880 football fans, how many do not support Manchester United?

a. 2420
b. 2640
c. 2680
d. 2740
e. 2520

5. A paramedic leaves the Ambulance Station at 08.00 hours and returns at 14.45 hours. How many hours has he been away from station?

a. 5 hours 50 minutes
b. 5 hours 45 minutes
c. 6 hours 50 minutes
d. 6 hours 45 minutes
e. 6 hours 15 minutes

6. You go to your local supermarket. You decide to buy some tomato soup. Each tin costs 14p. How much will 6 tins cost in total?

a. 60p
b. 64p
c. 70p
d. 84p
e. 86p

7. One carpet tile measures 50cm by 50cm. How many tiles are required to cover a floor which measures 10m by 2m?

a. 70
b. 75
c. 80
d. 85
e. 90

8. One power station supplies power to 34,000 homes. How many homes would 4 power stations supply?

a. 126,000
b. 128,000
c. 138,000
d. 148,000
e. 136,000

9. A drum contains 23 litres of oil. If a ship carries 11 drums of oil onboard, how many litres of oil are there altogether?

a. 233 litres
b. 241 litres
c. 253 litres
d. 263 litres
e. 266 litres

10. A football match has an average of 32,000 spectators. There are 26 football matches a year. What is the total number of spectators throughout the year?

a. 83,200
b. 832,000
c. 964,000
d. 110,600
e. 124,000

11. A library has 25 shelves of books. Each shelf holds 700 books. How many books are in the library?

a. 1,750
b. 17,050
c. 17,500
d. 35,000
e. 38,500

12. At an allotment there are 3 plots: plot A, plot B and plot C. Using the diagram below, calculate the area of plot B.

a. 1,000 m²
b. 2,500 m²
c. 2,000 m²
d. 3,000 m²
e. 100 m²

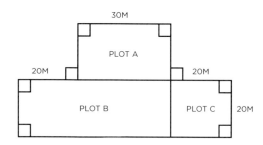

13. What is the average value of the following: 14, 28, 47, 47, 60 and 104?

a. 50
b. 53
c. 55
d. 60
e. 62

14. There are 44 police forces in the United Kingdom. Each police force has 14 Senior Officers. How many Senior Officers are there in total?

a. 561

b. 606

c. 616

d. 861

e. 882

15. A company has to dismiss 1 out of 6 of their employees. If the company employs 636 people, how many will the company have to dismiss?

a. 96

b. 103

c. 106

d. 126

e. 132

16. If 6 out of 24 emergency care assistants become paramedics, what is this as a fraction?

a. 1/4

b. 2/4

c. 1/8

d. 1/6

e. 1/3

17. You go to the local shop and buy a magazine costing £2.40 and a drink costing £1.12. How much change do you get from a £10 note?

a. £6.52

b. £4.48

c. £5.52

d. £6.48

e. £6.56

18. A cruise ship can carry 90,000 passengers. On this occasion the ship is only 75% full. How many passengers are on board?

a. 6,750

b. 13,500

c. 54,500

d. 67,500

e. 68,250

19. A car garage sells 50 cars per month. 2 % of these are returned with engine problems. How many cars with engine problems are returned to the car garage each year?

a. 6
b. 9
c. 13
d. 15
e. 12

20. A Formula 1 car drives 660 miles in 3 hours 40 minutes. What is its average speed?

a. 160 mph
b. 190 mph
c. 180 mph
d. 185 mph
e. 190 mph

21. You can run 2 miles in 18 minutes. How long does it take you to run 0.5 miles at this speed?

a. 4 minutes 30 seconds
b. 5 minutes
c. 6 minute 30 seconds
d. 4 minutes 20 seconds
e. 5 minutes 10 seconds

22. You walk to school and it takes you 20 minutes. You know that you walk an average of 3 mph. How far is school from your house?

a. 2 miles
b. 1 mile
c. 6 miles
d. 4 miles
e. 5 miles

23. A farmer has 650 sheep. He keeps his sheep in 5 large fields. How many sheep does he have in each field?

a. 120
b. 130
c. 150
d. 160
e. 170

24. A delivery driver has to drive on average 12,000 miles a month. If the driver works every day in April, how many miles does he have to drive each day?

a. 200 miles
b. 300 miles
c. 350 miles
d. 387 miles
e. 400 miles

25. You withdraw 30% of your savings from an account which holds £600. How much remains in the account?

a. £360
b. £390
c. £420
d. £430
e. £450

Now move on to practice test 5.

Practice Test 5

You have 12 minutes to complete 25 questions. Please circle the correct answer. You are not permitted to use a calculator at any point in the test.

1. A cruise ship has 13 rows of windows. If each row has 39 windows, how many windows are there in total?

a. 498
b. 507
c. 527
d. 618
e. 627

2. In a car park there are 325 cars, and each car has 4 tyres and 1 spare tyre. How many tyres are there throughout the car park?

a. 1,525
b. 1,575
c. 1,650
d. 1,675
e. 1,625

3. A greengrocer has a box of 360 strawberries. The greengrocer wants to make up punnets of strawberries, each with 36 strawberries in it. How many punnets of strawberries can the greengrocer make?

a. 6
b. 10
c. 12
d. 26
e. 36

4. A ball of wool measures 3.3 metres. If you have 100 balls of wool, how many metres will there be?

a. 3.30 metres
b. 33.0 metres
c. 330 metres
d. 3,300 metres
e. 660 metres

5. How many pieces of string measuring 1.25 metres in length can be cut from a ball which is 100m long?

a. 12.5
b. 125
c. 80
d. 250
e. 250

6. One case containing 42 cartons of orange juice costs £6.30. How much will two cartons of orange juice cost?

a. 10p
b. 15p
c. 25p
d. 30p
e. 45p

7. A moped is travelling at a speed of 35 mph. How long does it take to travel 7 miles?

a. 6 minutes
b. 10 minutes
c. 24 minutes
d. 8 minutes
e. 12 minutes

8. A train travels a total distance of 540 miles at a constant speed of 90 mph. How long does the journey last?

a. 360 minutes
b. 320 minutes
c. 240 minutes
d. 300 minutes

9. What speed do you need to travel to go 100 miles in 2 hours?

a. 25 mph
b. 200 mph
c. 10 mph
d. 20 mph
e. 50 mph

10. A prisoner has escaped from prison. The prison is 20 miles away. You need to get there in 15 minutes. How fast do you need to drive?

a. 40 mph
b. 60 mph
c. 80 mph
d. 85 mph
e. 90 mph

11. A CD album has 49 minutes worth of songs. If each song is 3 minutes 30 seconds long, how many songs are on the album?

a. 7
b. 14
c. 15
d. 28
e. 18

12. A coach driver is making a journey form Land's End to John O'Groats. This is a distance of 420 miles. He has to make 7 equal stops. How many miles apart does each stop have to be?

a. 60
b. 80
c. 45
d. 70
e. 50

13. A train has 6 trams and each tram holds 80 tonnes of freight. What is the total weight of freight carried by the train?

a. 380 tonnes
b. 420 tonnes
c. 480 tonnes
d. 570 tonnes
e. 580 tonnes

14. An office has 333 computer desks. If only 2/3 are used, how many are un-used?

a. 33
b. 90
c. 111
d. 222
e. 22

15. Mike cycles every day for 30 minutes. How much time does he spend cycling over 8 days?

a. 3.5 hours
b. 4 hours
c. 4.5 hours
d. 5 hours
e. 5.5 hours

16. A rugby club raises its annual subscription of £300 by 25%. What will the new subscription be?

a. £345
b. £360
c. £370
d. £375
e. £385

17. A cinema ticket costs £5.00. If a pensioner is given a 15% discount, how much change will they get from a £20 note?

a. £15.25
b. £15.45
c. £15.75
d. £16.25
e. £16.30

18. A circle has a diameter of 240 mm. What is the length, in centimetres, of the radius?

a. 12 cm
b. 18 cm
c. 22 cm
d. 6 cm
e. 24 cm

19. At the top of the next page is a bar chart showing yearly vegetable sales for a market in Castleton. What is the average yearly sale of mushrooms over the three years?

a. 200
b. 225
c. 250
d. 300
e. 350

YEARLY VEGETABLE SALES

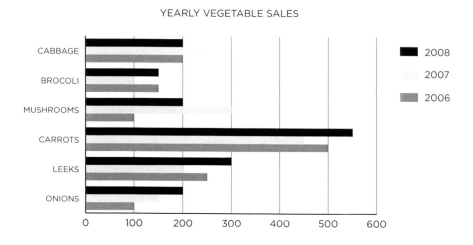

20. Roger needs to lay new turf in his garden. The whole of the garden will need new turf. Calculate the area of the garden that will need new turf.

a. 66 ft²
b. 112 ft²
c. 128 ft²
d. 132 ft²
e. 144 ft²

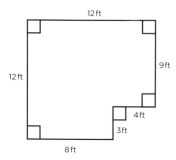

21. If I have £40 in my wallet and spend £13.75 of it, how much will I have left?

a. £25.75
b. £26.25
c. £27.50
d. £28.15
e. £29.60

22. A motorist is travelling at 80mph. How far will he have travelled in 15 minutes?

a. 10 miles
b. 15 miles
c. 12 miles
d. 25 miles
e. 20 miles

23. A prison cell holds two people. There are two prison areas: high risk and low risk. The high risk area has 123 cells and the low risk area has 334 cells. How many prisoners are there in the prison?

a. 897
b. 910
c. 914
d. 1,010
e. 1,028

24. A food processing company has 10 people a week absent due to illness. How many people are absent due to illness in a year?

a. 520
b. 730
c. 1,040
d. 3,640
e. 3,650

25. Balmoray Police operates a three-shift working pattern in each day. Each shift has to have 22 police officers on duty. How many officers are required for a days work?

a. 66
b. 62
c. 60
d. 86
e. 132

Now move on to practice test 6.

Practice Test 6

You have 12 minutes to complete 25 questions. Please circle the correct answer. You are not permitted to use a calculator at any point in the test.

1. In the Johnson family there are 7 people; 3 of them are female. What is this as a fraction?

a. 2/3
b. 4/6
c. 3/7
d. 6/15
e. 1/3

2. You are at a traffic collision where a vehicle has crashed into a play area. As part of your documentation you need to calculate the area of the playing field. Using the diagram below, work out the area of the playing field and select the appropriate answer.

a. 700 m²
b. 900 m²
c. 1,200 m²
d. 1,300 m²
e. 1,400 m²

3. Your yearly salary is £40,000. You also receive a yearly bonus which is 15% of your salary. How much do you earn per year?

a. £40,060
b. £40,600
c. £46,000
d. £49,000
e. £56,000

4. On a housing estate there are 34,000 homes. Of these homes 63% are semi-detached, 30% are detached, and the remainder are terraced houses. How many houses are terraced?

a. 23.8
b. 238
c. 2,380
d. 2,680
e. 23,800

5. You are a police officer and you have two foot patrols a day. The total distance walked is 20 miles. If you walked an average speed of 4 mph, how long is each patrol?

a. 5 hours
b. 3 hours 30 minutes
c. 4 hours
d. 2 hours 30 minutes
e. 4 hours 20 minutes

6. You are tasked to drive your boss to a meeting 100 miles away. You will be driving at 60 mph. If you set off at 10:20pm, what time would you arrive?

a. 11:40pm
b. 12:00pm
c. 12:40pm
d. 12:20pm
e. 12:30pm

7. A criminal sprints at a speed of 10 metres every 2 seconds (10m/ 2 seconds). How long does it take him to run 1,000 metres if he continues at the same speed?

a. 100 seconds
b. 10 seconds
c. 200 seconds
d. 20 seconds
e. 25 seconds

8. You are at a fruit and vegetable stall at a market. If one apple costs 41p, how much would it cost to buy 11 apples?

a. £4.41
b. £4.21
c. £4.61
d. £4.67
e. £4.51

9. A car garage orders four new sport cars costing £41,000 each.
How much in total has the garage spent on the new sports cars?

a. £124,000
b. £154,000
c. £164,000
d. £166,000
e. £168,000

10. A water tank has a maximum capacity of 200 litres. If the tank is 80%
full how many more litres are required to fill it to its maximum?

a. 25 litres
b. 40 litres
c. 50 litres
d. 55 litres
e. 60 litres

11. If I spend £1.60, £2.35, £3.55 and £4.75 on a selection of goods, how
much will I have spent in total?

a. £10.65
b. £11.60
c. £11.55
d. £12.25
e. £12.55

12. Below is a chart showing snowfall across the Lincolnshire region in
2004 in centimetres. What is the combined snowfall for January and May?

a. 5.5 cm
b. 6.0 cm
c. 6.5 cm
d. 7.0 cm
e. 8.5 cm

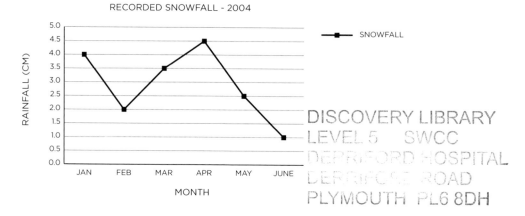

RECORDED SNOWFALL - 2004

SNOWFALL

RAINFALL (CM)

MONTH

13. On Monday it takes Lucy 52 minutes to get to work. On Tuesday it takes 40 minutes, Wednesday takes 51 minutes, on Thursday it takes 1 hour 2 minutes and on Friday it takes 1 hour 30 minutes. How long did her average commute take?

a. 58 minutes

b. 62 minutes

c. 60 minutes

d. 61 minutes

e. 59 minutes

14. Paul is a 100 metre sprinter. During a weekend-long competition he runs the distance in 11 seconds, 9 seconds, 9.5 seconds and 11.5 seconds. What is the average time that Paul runs 100 metres in?

a. 9 seconds

b. 10 seconds

c. 11 seconds

d. 10.25 seconds

e. 10.5 seconds

15. One in fourteen people become a victim of car crime each year. In Saxby there are 224 people. On that basis, how many people per year experience car crime in Saxby?

a. 14

b. 16

c. 18

d. 20

e. 22

16. Lisa's weekly newspaper bill is £5.50 and the delivery charge is 35p per week. How much does she have to pay over six weeks?

a. £28.10

b. £31.10

c. £35.10

d. £35.20

e. £36.10

17. A gardener wants to gravel over the area shown below. One bag of gravel will cover 20 m². How many bags are needed to cover the entire garden?

a. 40

b. 55

c. 65

d. 75

e. 130

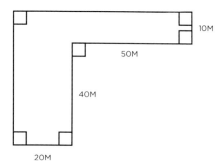

18. The gardener decides he is only going to gravel 20% of the garden. Using the above diagram, how many square metres will he be gravelling?

a. 26 m²

b. 300 m²

c. 130 m²

d. 240 m²

e. 260 m²

19. You stop and search 40 people, and 8 of them are arrested for possession of a class A drug. What is this as a fraction?

a. 1/3

b. 1/4

c. 1/6

d. 1/10

e. 1/5

20. There are 144 people entered into a raffle, 12 people each win a prize. What is this as a fraction?

a. 1/6

b. 1/8

c. 1/12

d. 1/24

e. 1/10

21. At a music festival there are 35,000 festival goers, 5% of these are under 16 years of age. How many festival goers were under 16?

a. 1500
b. 1750
c. 2500
d. 3500
e. 7000

22. At Christmas you buy 30 presents; 12 are bought for your family and 18 for your friends. What percentage was bought for your friends?

a. 20%
b. 30%
c. 40%
d. 60%
e. 75%

23. Over one year, the Ambulance Service attends 600 drink driving incidents. For recording purposes, these are divided into 5 piles dependent on how much over the limit the driver was. If the piles are all equal sizes, how many are in each pile?

a. 115 files
b. 120 files
c. 125 files
d. 130 files
e. 135 files

24. On average, 1 out of every 30 people experience back problems in their lifetime. Out of 900 people, how many will experience back problems?

a. 20
b. 30
c. 60
d. 90
e. 120

25. Below are a toy company's monthly sale figures. Calculate the average toy sales per month for the year.

a. 350
b. 375
c. 450
d. 500
e. 700

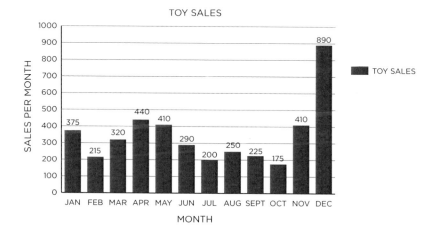

Now move on to practice test 7.

Practice Test 7

You have 12 minutes to complete 25 questions. Please circle the correct answer. You are not permitted to use a calculator at any point in the test.

1. Billy can run 1.5 miles in 12 minutes. How long does it take him to run 12 miles if he continues at the same speed?

a. 1 hour 26 minutes
b. 1 hour 12 minutes
c. 1 hour 36 minutes
d. 1 hour 6 minutes
e. 1 hour 20 minutes

2. Jennifer runs 39 miles in 4 hours 20 minutes. What was her average speed?

a. 12 mph
b. 10 mph
c. 9 mph
d. 7 mph
e. 8 mph

3. An emergency response helicopter flies a distance of 840 miles in 6 hours. What speed is it flying at in miles per hour?

a. 140 mph
b. 160 mph
c. 150 mph
d. 145 mph
e. 135 mph

4. Emma works 5 days a week. Everyday she drives 20 miles to work, and 20 miles back. She drives at an average speed of 30 mph. How much time does Emma spend driving to work and back each working week?

a. 6 hours 40 minutes
b. 6 hours 15 minutes
c. 6 hours 20 minutes
d. 6 hours 45 minutes
e. 7 hours

5. You are driving to an incident at 96 mph. The incident is 24 miles away. How long will it take you to get to the incident?

a. 12 minutes
b. 15 minutes
c. 10 minutes
d. 20 minutes
e. 25 minutes

6. You are driving at 42 mph for 20 minutes. How far have you come?

a. 14 miles
b. 20 miles
c. 17 miles
d. 15 miles
e. 16 miles

7. In a year 20,600 people are arrested. One quarter of these are over 50 years of age. How many people over 50 years of age are arrested?

a. 4,150
b. 4,300
c. 5,350
d. 5,200
e. 5,150

8. If 2 out of 10 entrants won at a dog show, how many would win if there were 100 entrants at the show?

a. 10
b. 15
c. 20
d. 35
e. 40

9. The pie chart at the top of the next page shows the percentage of aircraft sales across the world. If 10,000 aircraft were sold in total, how many were sold in the UK?

a. 15,000
b. 1,750
c. 150
d. 1,000
e. 1,500

AIRCRAFT SALES

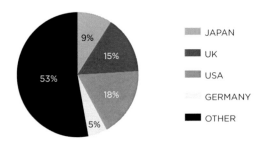

10. Using the pie chart above calculate, the combined aircraft sales for both the USA and other countries.

a. 710
b. 1,710
c. 1,900
d. 6,500
e. 7,100

11. Calculate the perimeter of the shape below.

a. 18.4 cm
b. 28.0 cm
c. 28.4 cm
d. 32.0 cm
e. 32.8 cm

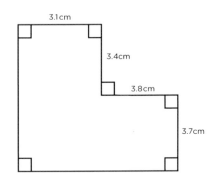

12. An office block has a length of 28 metres and width of 10 metres. What is the size of the floor space?

a. 176 m²
b. 240 m²
c. 280 m²
d. 440 m²
e. 560 m²

13. An office has a floor space of 21,000 m². If 700 people work in the office, how much m² space does each employee have?

a. 3 m²
b. 30 m²
c. 60 m²
d. 90 m²
e. 300 m²

14. New paramedic boots cost £112; you are subsidised £42 from the NHS Trust to contribute towards the boots. How much will you need to contribute?

a. £60
b. £62
c. £58
d. £74
e. £70

15. I have £13 in my wallet and spend £4.37 shopping. How much do I have left?

a. £8.73
b. £7.63
c. £8.63
d. £6.85
e. £6.53

16. How much do 24 boxes of chocolates cost at £4.10 each?

a. £98.20
b. £78.20
c. £88.40
d. £94.40
e. £98.40

17. Police in Horncastle pull over 200 suspected drink drivers over a 6 month period. There are 36 people over the drink driving limit. Out of the 200, what percentage are over the legal limit?

a. 16%
b. 18%
c. 24%
d. 30%
e. 36%

18. Each year 15,000 people are recruited into the Ambulance Service in Scotland. 30% are female employees. How many male employees are recruited in Scotland each year?

a. 4500
b. 7500
c. 10500
d. 12500
e. 15000

19. What is the average age of a group of children whose individual ages are 11 years, 13 years, 9 years, 9 years, and 8 years?

a. 10 years
b. 11 years
c. 12 years
d. 13 years
e. 14 years

20. How much would it cost to buy 26 jars of jam at £1.15 per jar?

a. £26.90
b. £27.60
c. £28.50
d. £29.45
e. £29.90

21. There are 635 boxes in a lorry. How many boxes would there be in 3 lorries?

a. 1,605
b. 1,805
c. 1,850
d. 1,905
e. 1,980

22. In a pick and mix you get 25 sweets in a bag for £4.00. How much does each sweet cost?

a. £0.10
b. £0.16
c. £1.00
d. £1.60
e. £1.80

23. You are trying to decide where to go on a skiing holiday. To fly to Tignes in France will take 3 hours 30 minutes; to fly to Whistler in Canada will take 6 hours 50 minutes; and to fly to Switzerland will take 4 hours 40 minutes. What is the average journey time for all three different routes?

a. 4 hours
b. 5 hours
c. 6 hours
d. 7 hours
e. 10 hours

24. PC Wood is carrying out research into the market value of narcotics. He is given four values for an eighth of an ounce of cannabis: £19, £22, £21.75, and £25.25. What is the average value for an eighth of an ounce of cannabis?

a. £17
b. £19
c. £21
d. £22
e. £24

25. Your business has yearly profits of £520,000. There are 13 equal share holders in the company. How much does each individual make in profit?

a. £20,000
b. £30,000
c. £35,000
d. £40,000
e. £42,000

Now move on to practice test 8.

Practice Test 8

You have 12 minutes to complete 25 questions. Please circle the correct answer. You are not permitted to use a calculator at any point in the test.

1. At a football tournament there are 15 teams. Each team has a squad of twenty players. How many players are there in total?

a. 200
b. 300
c. 400
d. 450
e. 500

2. The total number of hours worked by employees in a week is 390. If there are 13 employees, how many hours per work does each person work?

a. 3 hours
b. 20 hours
c. 30 hours
d. 45 hours
e. 60 hours

3. The diagram below shows a playing field and a sand pit. Calculate the area of the playing field using the information displayed.

a. 950 m²
b. 1,400 m²
c. 1,950 m²
d. 2,400 m²
e. 2,850 m²

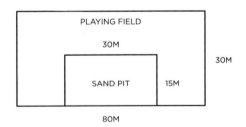

4. Hampshire Ambulance Service operate a three-shift working pattern each day. Each shift has to have 24 paramedics on duty. How many paramedics are required for a week's work, Monday to Friday?

a. 36
b. 480
c. 420
d. 504
e. 360

5. Below is a scatter graph portraying sample height and shoe size for Class 4 at Edgbaston Primary School. What is the combined average shoe size for someone who is 160 cm tall and someone who is 180 cm tall?

a. 6.25
b. 9
c. 7.5
d. 8.5
e. 7

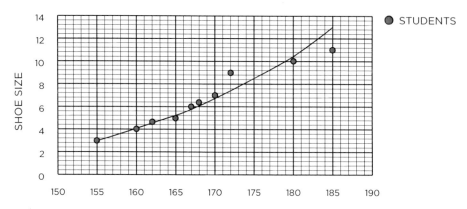

CLASS 4: SAMPLE HEIGHT & SHOE SIZE

6. Using the scatter graph (and trend line) above, calculate the approximate shoe size of a student who is 175 cm in height.

a. 7
b. 7.5
c. 8
d. 8.5
e. 9

7. You need to measure the perimeter of a square house. You know that one side of the house measures 15.5 metres. What is the perimeter of the house?

a. 52 metres
b. 62 metres
c. 63 metres
d. 64 metres
e. 66 metres

8. A paramedic has to put some marker cones out along a stretch of road. The road is 240 metres long and cones have to be placed 1.5 metres apart. How many cones will the paramedic need?

a. 150
b. 160
c. 165
d. 170
e. 180

9. The school run in Milton Keynes takes 3 minutes if you drive at a speed of 30 mph. How far away is the school?

a. 1½ miles
b. 2 miles
c. 3 miles
d. 5½ miles
e. 10 miles

10. You are flying at 240 mph. How far have you travelled in 12 minutes?

a. 24 miles
b. 48 miles
c. 36 miles
d. 20 miles
e. 40 miles

11. You have arrived at an RTA (Road Traffic Accident) and immediately call for the police. The police car is 12 miles from your current location. You have told the police that you need it here in 5 minutes. What speed must the police drive at to get to the RTA on time?

a. 60 mph
b. 140 mph
c. 50 mph
d. 144 mph
e. 132 mph

12. There are 18 strawberries in a punnet. In a shop there are 12 punnets. How many strawberries are there in total?

a. 132
b. 162
c. 316

 THE **TESTING** SERIES

d. 432

e. 216

13. You find a purse in the street. It contains a £10 note, a £5 note, four £2 coins, three £1 coins, a 50p coin, four 2p coins and a penny. How much is there in the purse?

a. £22.59

b. £22.49

c. £24.69

d. £25.69

e. £26.59

14. A car park in Warrington issues 15 parking fines a week, each costing £60. How much does the car park make from fines every 4 weeks?

a. £1,800

b. £2,600

c. £3,600

d. £3,800

e. £4,800

15. Mary goes food shopping 3 times a week. How many times does she go food shopping in a year?

a. 156

b. 158

c. 166

d. 226

e. 256

16. The plan below shows a layout of your garden and vegetable plot. You want to lay decking over half of the garden. What area will the decking cover?

a. 20 m²

b. 100 m²

c. 125 m²

d. 175 m²

e. 200 m²

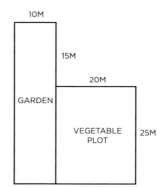

17. 15% of the vegetable plot is used to grow carrots. Using the above diagram calculate what area of the vegetable plot is used to grow carrots?

a. 25 m²
b. 37.5 m²
c. 48 m²
d. 50 m²
e. 75 m²

18. At Lowbridge High School there are 180 students taking exams. 60 of these students gain A to C grades. What is this as a fraction?

a. 1/4
b. 1/3
c. 2/3
d. 1/6
e. 1/5

19. Your family own 5 cars. 3 of the cars are red. What is this as a percentage?

a. 30%
b. 40%
c. 60%
d. 65%
e. 70%

20. Whilst shopping I spend £1.60, £2.35, £5.60 and 74p. How much have I spent in total?

a. £10.39
b. £10.29
c. £10.49
d. £10.59
e. £11.29

21. A car ownership survey discovered that out of 10,000 cars, 2,500 were Fords. What is this as a percentage?

a. 20%
b. 25%
c. 30%
d. 35%
e. 40%

22. A motorbike is speeding at 180 mph. How far does it travel in 10 minutes?

a. 60 miles
b. 40 miles
c. 30 miles
d. 25 miles
e. 20 miles

23. A train is travelling at a speed of 80 mph. The distance between station A and station B is 200 miles. How long will it take to get from station A to station B?

a. 2 hours 15 minutes
b. 2 hours 20 minutes
c. 2 hours 35 minutes
d. 2 hours 40 minutes
e. 2 hours 30 minutes

24. You are running late for work and you have 30 minutes to get there on time. Your work is 25 miles away. What speed do you have to drive at so as not to be late?

a. 75 mph
b. 45 mph
c. 50 mph
d. 30 mph
e. 15 mph

25. What speed would you need travel at to achieve 180 miles in 20 minutes?

a. 360 mph
b. 540 mph
c. 270 mph
d. 90 mph
e. 100 mph

Now move on to practice test 9.

Practice Test 9

You have 12 minutes to complete 25 questions. Please circle the correct answer. You are not permitted to use a calculator at any point in the test.

1. As a paramedic you cover 360 miles a day. Over an 8-hour shift, what is your average speed for the day?

a. 50 mph
b. 60 mph
c. 48 mph
d. 45 mph
e. 46 mph

2. A journey takes 2 hours and 30 minutes. You have been travelling at a speed of 70 mph. How far have you travelled?

a. 160 miles
b. 170 miles
c. 175 miles
d. 185 miles
e. 190 miles

3. A garage is selling three used cars. The mileage on the first is 119,500; the mileage on the second is 140,500; the mileage on the third in 160,000. What is the average mileage of the three used cars?

a. 140,000
b. 142,000
c. 145,000
d. 150,000
e. 135,000

4. At a restaurant you and your friend buy a king prawn salad (£6.95), some salmon fish cakes (£5.95), steak and chips (£11.50), chicken and chips (£10.25) and a chocolate cake (£3.95). You agree to split the bill equally. How much do you both pay?

a. £19.50
b. £19.40
c. £19.30
d. £19.20
e. £19.10

 THE **TESTING** SERIES

5. In a restaurant you and your friend buy a salad (£3.95), scallops (£6.95), steak and chips (£12.60), chicken and chips (£9.15) and ice cream (£1.95). You agree to split the bill equally, how much do you both pay?

a. £17.35
b. £18.40
c. £17.60
d. £15.30
e. £17.30

6. A company adds up the total number of sick days had by its employees. Out of the 52 weeks in a year it is calculated that, in total, employees have 13 weeks off sick. What is this as a percentage?

a. 25%
b. 20%
c. 15%
d. 10%
e. 5%

7. Using the diagram below, calculate the perimeter of the lily bed.

a. 70 m
b. 75 m
c. 90 m
d. 95 m
e. 100 m

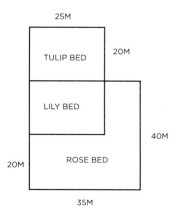

8. A bag contains 5 litres of compost soil. You calculate that 5 litres of compost will cover an area of 2.5 m². Using the above diagram calculate how many bags of soil you will need to fill the tulip bed.

a. 20 bags
b. 100 bags
c. 200 bags
d. 250 bags
e. 400 bags

9. If the police air support unit flies at a speed of 120 mph for 12 minutes, how far has it travelled?

a. 48 miles
b. 26 miles
c. 12 miles
d. 24 miles
e. 6 miles

10. A bus drives for 4 hours covering a total distance of 240 miles. What was his average speed in miles per hour?

a. 120 mph
b. 30 mph
c. 40 mph
d. 60 mph
e. 50 mph

11. Five out of one hundred police officers are injured during duty every year. What is this as a fraction?

a. 1/5
b. 1/20
c. 1/30
d. 2/50
e. 1/4

12. School dinners cost £4.75 each, and 200 children have dinners each day. How much is made from school dinners per day?

a. £550
b. £750
c. £850
d. £950
e. £1,050

13. You have a meeting at 0900hrs. You leave your house at 0840hrs. The meeting location from your house is 20 miles away. It will take you 5 minutes to walk from your car to the meeting room. What speed must you drive at to ensure you are on time?

a. 70 mph
b. 65 mph
c. 80 mph

d. 75 mph

e. 60 mph

14. Farmer Sid collects bales of hay during his autumn harvest. In his first field he collects 43, in his second field he collects 62, in his third field he collects 13 and in his fourth field he collects 42. What is the average number of hay bales he collects from his fields?

a. 39

b. 40

c. 41

d. 42

e. 37

15. There are four new paramedic recruits Mark, Laura, Ryan and Amy. Mark is 2 metres tall, Laura is 1.7 metres tall, Ryan is 1.8 metres tall, and Amy is 1.5 metres tall. What is the average height of the recruits in metres?

a. 1.77 metres

b. 1.68 metres

c. 1.62 metres

d. 1.70 metres

e. 1.75 metres

16. Below is a bar chart showing daily book sales for four stores. How many books in total does Jay's Books sell.

a. 40

b. 45

c. 50

d. 55

e. 60

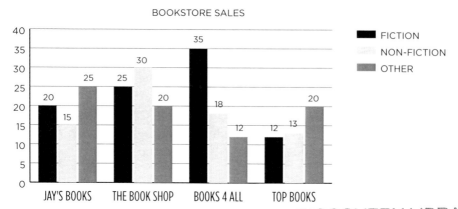

BOOKSTORE SALES

FICTION
NON-FICTION
OTHER

17. What, on average, is the total amount of books sold at The Book Shop and Top Books?

a. 50
b. 55
c. 60
d. 75
e. 90

18. Whilst shopping you buy 6 items. You buy a steak costing £12.50, some vegetables costing £5.75, some cereal costing £1.21, some wine costing £10, some shampoo costing 42p and finally some sweets costing 12p. What is the average cost of the items you buy?

a. £4
b. £5
c. £6
d. £7
e. £8

19. The distance between A and B is 140 miles. It takes you 4 hours to drive the distance. What speed have you been travelling at?

a. 70 mph
b. 40 mph
c. 35 mph
d. 30 mph
e. 25 mph

20. You must arrive at work at 0900hrs. Your house is 6 miles from work. If you were to drive at 30 mph, what time would you need to leave the house to arrive at work on time?

a. 0847hrs
b. 0857hrs
c. 0848hrs
d. 0842hrs
e. 0838hrs

21. On a Saturday night the police arrest 40 people. 22 are arrested for being drunk and disorderly, 10 are arrested for assault and 8 are arrested for drink driving. What percentage have been arrested for drink driving?

a. 2%
b. 5%
c. 10%
d. 20%
e. 25%

22. During a walk you average 12 miles at 3 mph. How long would it take to do a 14-mile walk?

a. 4 hours 50 minutes
b. 4 hours 45 minutes
c. 4 hours 20 minutes
d. 4 hours 35 minutes
e. 4 hours 40 minutes

23. A train is travelling from Birmingham to Glasgow covering a distance of 390 miles. If the train's speed is 90 mph, how long does the train journey last?

a. 4 hours 20 minutes
b. 4 hours 40 minutes
c. 4 hours 10 minutes
d. 4 hours 15 minutes
e. 4 hours 30 minutes

24. You have 225 bags of sugar. If 15 bags of sugar fit in a box, how many boxes would you have in total?

a. 10
b. 12
c. 13
d. 15
e. 20

25. Whilst hiking you walk a total distance of 725 miles over a 5-day period. On average, how many miles did you walk a day?

a. 145 miles
b. 150 miles
c. 125 miles
d. 90 miles
e. 160 miles

Now move on to practice test 10.

Practice Test 10

You have 12 minutes to complete 25 questions. Please circle the correct answer. You are not permitted to use a calculator at any point in the test.

1. An aircraft travels at a speed of 120 miles per hour over a total distance of 240 miles. How long does the journey take?

a. 2 hours
b. 4 hours
c. 3 hours
d. 2 hours 30 minutes
e. 1 hour

2. How long does it take to drive 20 miles if you drive at a speed of 30 mph?

a. 1 hour
b. 20 minutes
c. 40 minutes
d. 45 minutes
e. 50 minutes

3. A paramedic walks for 15 miles in 3 hours. At what speed does the paramedic walk?

a. 45 mph
b. 5 mph
c. 20 mph
d. 15 mph
e. 10 mph

4. The distance between campsite A and campsite B is 32 miles. You walk at an average speed of 6 mph. If you set off from campsite A at 0900hrs, what time would you arrive at campsite B?

a. 1520hrs
b. 1410hrs
c. 1440hrs
d. 1610hrs
e. 1420hrs

5. A train from Doncaster to Grimsby takes 1 hour 30 minutes. If the train is travelling at 64 mph, what is the distance travelled?

a. 94 miles
b. 96 miles
c. 95 miles
d. 92 miles
e. 98miles

6. A yacht sails at 30 mph. You are sailing across the Channel estuary which is 240 miles long. How long does it take you complete your journey?

a. 8 hours
b. 5 hours
c. 6 hours
d. 4 hours
e. 12 hours

7. You find a rucksack full of money. In the bag there is a bundle of fifty £10 notes, a bundle of twenty £5 notes and ten money bags of £2 coins, each containing 15 coins. What is the total amount in the rucksack?

a. 600
b. 750
c. 825
d. 900
e. 950

8. You annual car insurance costs £240.48. How much is this per month?

a. £20.04
b. £20.02
c. £18.04
d. £22.02
e. £22.06

9. During a week of action, the Police carry out four early morning drug raids. On Monday they enter a property at 0710hrs and leave at 0720hrs. On Tuesday they enter at 0810hrs and leave at 0840hrs; on Thursday they enter at 0850hrs and leave at 0905hrs; and on Friday they enter a property at 0700hrs and leave at 0725hrs. What was the average time spent at a property during these raids?

a. 10 minutes
b. 25 minutes
c. 20 minutes
d. 30 minutes
e. 45 minutes

10. The diagram below shows the floor plan of a house. Using the information supplied calculate the internal area of the house.

a. 880m2

b. 900 m2

c. 1,155 m2

d. 1,200 m2

e. 1,245 m2

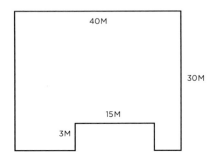

11. Using the plan above, calculate the perimeter of the house.

a. 145m

b. 146m

c. 148m

d. 152m

e. 156m

12. The train to work travels at 70 mph. The distance the train travels is 21 miles. How long does it take to travel to work?

a. 12 minutes

b. 8 minutes

c. 18 minutes

d. 15 minutes

e. 16 minutes

13. In your money box there are two £5 notes, five £2 coins, three £1 coins, six 10p coins and one penny. How much is in your money box?

a. £23.61

b. £13.61

c. £14.61

d. £16.41

e. £23.41

14. A room is 12 metres long and 5 metres wide. A carpet tile is 100cm by 100cm. How many tiles do you need to carpet the entire room?

a. 30

b. 40

c. 20

d. 6

e. 60

15. Bread costs £1.25, milk costs £2.13 and a pack of apples cost 66p. How much change will you have from £5?

a. £0.94

b. £0.96

c. £1.06

d. £1.36

e. £1.96

16. A TV has been reduced by 20% to £200. What was its original price?

a. £220

b. £240

c. £235

d. £250

e. £300

17. In Year 1 you had £200 in savings; by Year 2 this has increased to £230. By what percentage have your savings increased?

a. 10%

b. 12%

c. 15%

d. 20%

e. 25%

18. House prices have decreased by 5%. The price of your house before the decrease was £150,000. What is its price now?

a. £142,500

b. £143,000

c. £145,000

d. £146,000

e. £147,500

19. A car park has 8 floors. When completely full, each floor can hold 230 cars. How many cars in total can fit in the car park?

a. 1,440

b. 1,840

c. 2,040

d. 2,100

e. 2,140

20. A paramedic works 4 day shifts per week. How many days does a paramedic (without holiday entitlement) work a year?

a. 182

b. 192

c. 204

d. 206

e. 208

21. In one year a police officer arrests 321 people. 119 of these people are charged and the rest are cautioned. How many people are cautioned?

a. 202

b. 198

c. 200

d. 204

e. 206

22. John is 6ft 2", Ben is 5ft 9", Sarah is 5ft 4" and Garry is 5ft 7". What is the average height of the group?

a. 5ft 6"

b. 5ft 7.5"

c. 5ft 8.5"

d. 5ft 9"

e. 5ft"

23. A farmer has 5 identical fields, all of which are square fields. If one side of a field measures 500 metres long, what is the combined total perimeter of all the farmer's fields?

a. 1,000m

b. 10,000m

c. 25,000m

d. 50,000m

e. 100,000m

24. In a car park there are 1,200 cars. One sixth of the cars in the car park

are blue. How many are blue?

a. 20
b. 100
c. 200
d. 250
e. 400

25. In another car park there are 120 cars. Five tenths of the cars in the car park are red. Two thirds of the red cars have five doors. How many red cars have five doors?

a. 40
b. 30
c. 20
d. 70
e. 15

Now check your answer to the tests on the following page.

NUMERICAL REASONING PRACTICE TEST ANSWERS

Question No.	TEST 1	TEST 2	TEST 3	TEST 4	TEST 5	TEST 6	TEST 7	TEST 8	TEST 9	TEST 10
1	A	A	D	A	B	C	C	B	D	A
2	A	E	B	B	E	B	C	C	C	C
3	D	B	C	E	B	C	A	C	A	B
4	B	A	C	B	C	C	A	E	C	E
5	E	C	A	D	C	D	B	E	E	B
6	B	B	D	D	D	B	A	C	A	A
7	C	A	B	C	E	C	E	B	C	D
8	B	B	A	E	A	E	C	B	C	A
9	B	C	E	C	E	C	E	A	D	C
10	C	B	D	B	C	B	E	B	D	C
11	C	B	B	C	B	D	B	D	B	B
12	E	A	A	A	A	C	C	E	D	C
13	B	E	B	A	C	E	B	E	C	A
14	E	C	E	C	C	D	E	C	B	E
15	B	D	B	C	B	B	C	A	E	B
16	B	C	A	A	D	C	E	E	E	B
17	E	E	A	D	C	D	B	E	C	C
18	C	D	B	D	A	B	C	B	B	A
19	A	C	D	E	A	E	A	C	C	B
20	D	C	E	C	D	C	E	B	C	E
21	C	B	B	A	B	B	D	B	D	A
22	B	A	D	B	E	D	B	C	E	C
23	D	D	B	B	C	B	B	E	A	B
24	D	A	C	E	A	B	D	C	D	C
25	B	E	C	C	A	A	D	B	A	A

CHAPTER 3
VERBAL REASONING TESTS

As part of the selection process you may be required to sit a verbal reasoning test. Part of the role of a paramedic requires you to understand, analyse and interpret written information that is of a complex or specialised nature.

Within this section I have provided you a number of verbal reasoning tests to assist you during your preparation.

Exercise 1 consists of 30 multiple choice sample test questions. You have 9 minutes in which to complete the exercise.

The answers are provided at the end of the exercise.

VERBAL REASONING EXERCISE 1

1. Which of the following words is the odd one out?

a. Car
b. Aeroplane
c. Train
d. Bicycle
e. House

Answer ☐

2. Which of the following is the odd one out?

a. Right
b. White
c. Dart
d. Bright
e. Sight

Answer ☐

3. The following sentence has one word missing. Which ONE word makes the best sense of the sentence?

The mechanic worked on the car for three hours. At the end of the three hours he was _____ .

a. Home
b. Rich
c. Crying
d. Exhausted
e. Thinking

Answer ☐

4. The following sentence has 2 words missing. Which TWO words make best sense of the sentence?

The man _____ to walk along the beach with his dog. He threw the stick and the dog _____ it.

a. Hated/Chose
b. Decided/Wanted
c. Liked/Chased
d. Hurried/Chased
e. Hated/Loved

Answer [ ]

5. In the line below, the word outside of the brackets will only go with four of the words inside the brackets to make longer words. Which ONE word will it not go with?

	a.	b.	c.	d.
In	(direct	famous	describable	cart)

Answer [ ]

6. In the line below, the word outside of the brackets will only go with four of the words inside the brackets to make longer words. Which ONE word will it NOT go with?

	a.	b.	c.	d.
In	(decisive	reference	destructible	convenience)

Answer [ ]

7. In the line below, the word outside of the brackets will only go with four of the words inside the brackets to make longer words. Which ONE word will it NOT go with?

	a.	b.	c.	d.
A	(float	bout	part	peck)

Answer [ ]

8. Which of the following words is the odd one out?

a. Pink
b. Salt
c. Ball
d. Red
e. Grey

Answer

9. Which of the following words is the odd one out?

a. Run
b. Jog
c. Walk
d. Sit
e. Sprint

Answer

10. Which of the following words is the odd one out?

a. Eagle
b. Plane
c. Squirrel
d. Cloud
e. Bird

Answer

11. Which of the following words is the odd one out?

a Gold
b. Ivory
c. Platinum
d. Bronze
e. Silver

Answer

 THE **TESTING** SERIES

12. Which of the following is the odd one out?

a. Pond
b. River
c. Stream
d. Brook
e. Ocean

Answer [　　　]

13. Which of the following is the odd one out?

a. Wood
b. Chair
c. Table
d. Cupboard
e. Stool

Answer [　　　]

14. Which three-letter word can be placed in front of the following words to make a new word?

Time   Break   Light   Dreamer

Answer [　　　　　]

15. Which four-letter word can be placed in front of the following words to make a new word?

Box   Bag   Age   Card

Answer [　　　　　]

16. The following sentence has one word missing. Which ONE word makes the best sense of the sentence?

After walking for an hour in search of the pub, David decided it was time to turn _____ and go back home.

a. Up
b. In
c. Home
d. Around
e. Through

Answer [ ]

17. The following sentence has one word missing. Which ONE word makes the best sense of the sentence?

We are continually updating the site and would be _____ to hear any comments you may have.

a. Pleased   b. Worried   c. Available   d. Suited   e. Scared

Answer [ ]

18. The following sentence has two words missing. Which TWO words make the best sense of the sentence?

The Fleet Air Arm is the Royal Navy's air force. It numbers some 6200 people, _____ is 11.5% of the _____ Royal Naval strength.

a. which/total
b. and/total
c. which/predicted
d. and/corporate
e. which/approximately

Answer [ ]

19. The following sentence has one word missing. Which ONE word makes the best sense of the sentence?

The Navy has had to _____ and progress to be ever prepared to defend the British waters from rival forces.

a. Develop
b. Manoeuvre
c. Change

 THE **TESTING** SERIES

d. Seek

e. Watch

Answer [   ]

20. Which of the following is the odd one out?

a. Cat

b. Dog

c. Hamster

d. Owl

e. Rabbit

Answer [   ]

21. Which word best fits the following sentence?

My doctor says I_____ smoke. It's bad for my health.

a. Cannot

b. Wouldn't

c. Shouldn't

d. Like

e. Might

Answer [   ]

22. Which word best fits the following exercise?

The best thing for a hangover is to go to bed and sleep it _____ .

a. Through

b. Over

c. Away

d. In

e. Off

Answer [   ]

23. Complete the following sentence:

When Jane arrived at the disco, Andrew _____ .

a. Hadn't gone
b. Already left
c. Has already Left
d. Had not left
e. Had already left

Answer

24. Which of the following words is the odd one out?

a. Lawnmower
b. Hose
c. Rake
d. Carpet
e. Shovel

Answer

25. Complete the following sentence:

Karla was offered the job _____ having poor qualifications.

a. Although
b. Even though
c. With
d. Without
e. Despite

Answer

26. Complete the following sentence:

Not only _____ to Glasgow, but he also visited many other places in Scotland too.

a. Did she
b. Did he
c. Did he go
d. She went
e. She saw

Answer

27. Complete the following sentence:

Now please remember, you ―――――――― the test until the teacher tells you to.

a. Shouldn't
b. Cannot be starting
c. Are not to
d. Can't
e. Are not to start

Answer ☐

28. Which of the following is the odd one out?

a. Strawberry
b. Raspberry
c. Peach
d. Blackberry
e. Blueberry

Answer ☐

29. Which of the following is the odd one out?

a. Football
b. Wrestling
c. Table tennis
d. Golf
e. Rugby

Answer ☐

30. Which of the following is the odd one out?

a. Man
b. Milkman
c. Secretary
d. Policeman
e. Firefighter

Answer ☐

Now check your answers before moving on to the next exercise.

ANSWERS TO VERBAL REASONING EXERCISE 1

1. e	16. d
2. c	17. a
3. d	18. a
4. c	19. a
5. d	20. d
6. b	21. c
7. d	22. e
8. d	23. e
9. d	24. d
10. c	25. e
11. b	26. c
12. a	27. e
13. a	28. c
14. Day	29. b
15. Post	30. a

VERBAL REASONING EXERCISE 2

Now that you have completed exercise 1 take a look at exercise 2, which is of a different nature.

Take a look at the following example question:

Choose the word that best completes the following sentence:

The men _____ football until the sun went down.

a. kicked
b. played
c. lost
d. won
e. decided

The answer to the above questions is B.

Now take a look at the sample questions on the following pages.

Allow yourself 10 minutes to answer the 30 questions.

VERBAL REASONING EXERCISE 2

1. Insert the missing word:

If you are _____ at the written tests you will progress to the next stage.

a. Okay
b. Fail
c. Work
d. Successful
e. Pass

Answer [ ]

2. Hot is to cold as wet is to?

a. Dry
b. Water
c. Slippery
d. Wash
e. Lake

Answer [ ]

3. 'Bona fide' means the same as?

a. Correct
b. Genuine
c. Guessing
d. Caring
e. Want

Answer [ ]

4. Which of the following words is the closest to Horizontal?

a. Narrow
b. Vertical
c. Parallel
d. Round
e. Upwards

 THE **TESTING** SERIES

Answer ☐

5. Insert the missing word:

After satisfactory _____ of the medical, you will be measured for your uniform.

a. Pass
b. Sample
c. Attendance
d. Completion
e. Being

Answer ☐

6. Listen is to hear as Talk is to?

a. Watch
b. Mouth
c. Write
d. Say
e. Speak

Answer ☐

7. Which of the following words is closest to Gather?

a. Convene
b. Around
c. Stay
d. Refute
e. Disembark

Answer ☐

8. Insert the missing word:

In order to _____ the machinery you need to be qualified.

a. Direct
b. Operate

c. Qualify

d. Change

e. Assessed

Answer [   ]

9. Insert the missing word:

There are two aspects to _____ good habits.

a. Organising

b. Unfolding

c. Making

d. Developing

e. Start

Answer [   ]

10. Skilful means the same as?

a. Creative

b. Adept

c. Efficient

d. Working

e. Watchful

Answer [   ]

11. Car is to drive as Aeroplane is to?

a. Holiday

b. Cabin Crew

c. Airport

d. Fly

e. Wing

Answer [   ]

12. Tall is to short as Big is to?

a. Small
b. Length
c. Line
d. Thinner
e. Metre

Answer [   ]

13. Train is to track as Ship is to?

a. Harbour
b. Sea
c. Sail
d. Stern
e. Hull

Answer [   ]

14. If the following words were arranged in alphabetical order, which one would be second?

a. Believe
b. Beast
c. Belief
d. Bereaved
e. Best

Answer [   ]

15. If the following words were arranged in alphabetical order, which one would be last?

a. Desire
b. Desired
c. Desirable
d. Deserted
e. Desert

Answer [   ]

16. Walk is to run as Slow is to?

a. Fast
b. Speed
c. Quicker
d. Pace
e. Stop

Answer [   ]

17. Sun is to hot as Ice is to?

a. Melt
b. Winter
c. Icicle
d. Freeze
e. Cold

Answer [   ]

18. Which of the following words is closest to the word Tentative?

a. Caring
b. Desire
c. Watching
d. Hesitant
e. Scared

Answer [   ]

19. Which of the following words is closest to Regulate?

a. Signal
b. Direct
c. Control
d. Change
e. Assess

Answer [   ]

20. Hair is to head as Shoe is to?

a. Foot
b. Slipper
c. Glove
d. Laces
e. Heel

Answer [ ]

21. Insert the missing word:

James _____ the train and sat in First Class.

a. Climbed
b. Missed
c. Ran
d. Followed
e. Boarded

Answer [ ]

22. Which of the following words is closest to the meaning of Desire?

a. Achieve
b. Wish
c. Get
d. Ascertain
e. Believe

23. Hammer is to nail as Bat is to?

a. Fly
b. Ball
c. Cricket
d. Cat
e. Hit

Answer [ ]

24. Book is to read as Music is to?

a. Note
b. Instrument
c. Listen
d. Dance
e. Piano

Answer ☐

25. Which of the following words contains the most vowels?

a. Reasonable
b. Combination
c. Vegetables
d. Audaciously

Answer ☐

26. Which of the following words contains the least vowels?

a. Barber
b. Radio
c. Disastrous
d. Elephant
e. March

Answer ☐

27. Chair is to sit as Ladder is to?

a. Climb
b. Step
c. Bridge
d. Metal
e. Heavy

Answer ☐

28. Mark can run faster than Jane. Jane can run faster than Nigel who is slower than Bill. Bill runs faster than Mark. Who is the slowest?

a. Nigel
b. Jane
c. Bill
d. Mark

Answer ☐

29. If the following words were placed in alphabetical order, which one would be third?

a. Delightful
b. Delicious
c. Delayed
d. Delicate
e. Derail

Answer ☐

30. Insert the missing word:

Provisional offers of employment are made subject to _____ of references.

a. Receipt
b. Obtain
c. Gathering
d. Maintenance
e. The

Answer ☐

Now check your answers before moving on to the next exercise.

ANSWERS TO VERBAL REASONING EXERCISE 2

1. d	16. c
2. a	17. e
3. b	18. d
4. c	19. c
5. d	20. a
6. e	21. e
7. a	22. b
8. b	23. b
9. d	24. c
10. b	25. d
11. d	26. e
12. a	27. a
13. b	28. a
14. c	29. b
15. b	30. a

VERBAL REASONING COMPREHENSION EXERCISE

Another form of verbal reasoning assessment is the comprehension exercise.

This test usually includes a number of short passages of text followed by statements based on the information given in the passage. You are required to indicate whether the statements are true, false or cannot say, based on the information provided. When responding to these questions, use only the information provided in the passage and do not try to answer them in the light of any more detailed knowledge that you personally may have.

Take a look at the following sample question

SAMPLE QUESTION

Read the following passage before answering the question as true, false or cannot say.

Self-discipline is a crucial element to the role of a paramedic. Without self-discipline the paramedic will not perform his or her role competently. In relation to 'self-discipline' the paramedic must be committed to keeping up to date with policies, procedures and also their own continuous professional development. In addition to these important areas they must also be committed to upholding the values of the ambulance Service and maintain a high standard of work at all times.

Question 1

In order to maintain self-discipline the paramedic must be committed to keeping up to date with policies.

Answer: | TRUE | Based on the information provided the answer is true.

Now try the following sample questions. Remember to base your answers solely on the information provided in each passage. There are ten exercises in total and you have twenty minutes in which to complete them.

VERBAL REASONING COMPREHENSION EXERCISE

Read the following passage before answering the questions as either true, false or cannot say.

A paramedic is a health care professional in the senior ambulance service. They deal with accident and medical emergencies. They may work on their own, with the ambulance technician or an emergency care assistant meaning that they are one of a two person ambulance crew. In other circumstances a paramedic may be seen on their own, for example on a motor bike or in an emergency response car and occasionally a bicycle. When a paramedic is dealing with an accident or medical emergency their role is to review the patient's condition and give treatment that is essential to the individual. By assessing the patient's condition and deciding which treatment should be given before the patient is taken to hospital can potentially be a life-saving decision. With the assistance and help of an ambulance technician or emergency care assistant they will then begin to give necessary treatment to the patient. A paramedic uses specific techniques and procedures to try and resuscitate or stabilise the patient, using medical equipment and drugs that are within the ambulance vehicle. A paramedic is also trained to drive the ambulance vehicle, safely and effectively. Paramedic's work closely with other health care professionals such as nurses and doctors within the accident and emergency department of the hospital. The paramedic will brief the other members of the health professional team about the patient that they are transferring over to them. Paramedics will often work with other public services teams such as the police and the fire brigade. They may also deal with aggressive or hysterical members of the public and friends or family members who are at the scene of the emergency were their patient is. It is essential that a paramedic has knowledge about medication and how to apply their knowledge into their practical work; therefore a paramedic should be a confident person who can work with a high amount of responsibility and who can work to the challenge.

A paramedic must obtain mathematic skills to help when giving the correct dosage of medication, also when reading temperature must know how to convert centigrade to Fahrenheit. They must have the knowledge and skills to be able to use advanced life support systems and supplies. A paramedic

must be able to remain calm whilst working in challenging and stressful circumstances, ensuring they can stay focused. A paramedic needs to have excellent judgement skills along with a high level of knowledge and good technical skills, as these are important when directing other team members to assist. Providing top quality care and being able to handle high levels of stress are also part of being a good paramedic. Paramedics often respond to adverse and dangerous situations thus self-confidence is essential to have whilst being in the job role along with emotional stability, intellectual and cognitive requirements, tolerance for high stress and the ability to meet the physical demands also.

Question 1

Self-confidence is not required when working as a Paramedic.

Answer [   ]

Question 2

The colour of a Paramedics uniform is green.

Answer [   ]

Question 3

It is essential that a paramedic has knowledge about meditation.

Answer [   ]

Question 4

Handling high levels of stress is part of being a good paramedic.

Answer [   ]

VERBAL REASONING COMPREHENSION EXERCISE

Read the following passage before answering the questions as either true, false or cannot say.

All over the country the ambulance service can be reached by dialling 999. The ambulance and paramedic team are called out at all times of the day and all over the country. They may be called to a scene of an accident and this is when their experience, skills and quick thinking are used to ensure they arrive at the scene promptly. The paramedics will then look at the accident scene and start to treat the most severely injured first. They also have a responsibility to try and calm the other injured individuals that may be involved in the incident. It is extremely important that an ambulance crew are able to take care of the situation immediately whilst remaining in control and calm themselves. The paramedic team will usually carry out some basic first aid if needed and diagnostic tests at the scene. They also make the decision whether the patient can be dealt with on the scene or if they need transporting to the nearest hospital. The paramedics and ambulance technicians are highly skilled in advanced driving; therefore, they are able to move people away from the accident safely. The ambulance is known as transportation for sick or injured people to or from and between places of treatment. The word ambulance is Latin and comes from the word ambulare, which means to walk or move about. During the American Civil War ambulances were referred to as ambulance wagons. However, the history of the ambulance began in ancient times when they used carts to transport patients. The ambulance was first used for emergency transport in 1487 by the Spanish. With advances in technology throughout the 19th and 20th century this has led to our modern self-powered ambulances. There are many types of Ambulance vehicles such as the van or pick-up truck and car. In some areas motorcycles are used as they can travel through heavy traffic much faster than a van or a car. Helicopters are also used to reach places inaccessible by roads and where speed is of the essence. There are also boats and ships that are used in case of emergency at sea. Each ambulance has a wide variety of equipment on board. They have a two-way radio which allows them to receive and give information to and from the hospital and control panels. Some ambulances are fitted with mobile

data terminals. These are connected wirelessly to a central computer at the control centre to exchange important information. Some ambulances are also fitted with evidence gathering CCTV. These video cameras are used to record activity either inside or outside the vehicle, some also have sound recording facilities. This can be used as protection for the ambulance crews protecting them against violence or to prove or disprove cases where a member of crew stands accused of malpractice. Ambulances are fitted with a ramp or tail lift to help loading a patient; this prevents them from having to undertake any heavy lifting. The ramp is extremely important when loading onto the vehicle any heavy or bulky equipment such as hospital beds and even obese patients. Air conditioning is also fitted in the ambulance to help maintain an appropriate temperature for any patients being treated. Data recorders are also on-board ambulances to record information such as speed, braking power and time, emergency warning lights and sirens and also seat belt usage. These are usually used in coordination with GPS units. The ambulance also has a brightly coloured reflective appearance, markings, lights and audible warnings to ensure all other road users are aware of them. There are many different types of equipment and supplies kept on an ambulance such as ventilation and airway equipment, monitoring and defibrillation equipment, immobilisation devices, bandages, communication equipment, obstetrical kit, miscellaneous supplies, infection control equipment, injury prevention equipment. There is also the optional equipment and optional advanced equipment and medication. There are also many more supplies kept on board in an ambulance to ensure that the crew have the best equipment to deal with the situation they are in.

Question 5

The ambulance was first used for emergency transport in 1847 by the Spanish.

Answer [   ]

Question 6

The word ambulare is Latin and comes from the word ambulance.

Answer [   ]

Question 7

Some Ambulances are fitted with CCTV for the sole purpose of protecting the crews from violence.

Answer [   ]

Question 8

GPS stands for Global Positioning System.

Answer [   ]

VERBAL REASONING COMPREHENSION EXERCISE

Read the following passage before answering the questions as either true, false or cannot say.

An emergency medical dispatcher works as part of the ambulance service trusts control team. This job role can sometimes be split into call takers and dispatchers. When this happens the call takers answer 999 calls from the public and GP's. They have to work quickly and calmly as they take essential details about the patient's condition and the exact location of the patient; they then log the details onto a computer system. The information collected is then passed onto the emergency dispatcher. This is an important process as the emergency dispatcher uses this information to make important decisions about what is the best way to handle the situation. When the roles are combined together, the emergency medical dispatchers have to answer urgent calls that are made to the control centre. They are then working under the direction of the control officer. They take the essential details needed and decide on the type of action that is needed to be taken and if needed, they dispatch the nearest ambulance, rapid car response, motorcycle or paramedic helicopter. This is a high pressured role as they have to ensure the best possible use is made of all resources and that the high standards of the response times are met. When taking important information from a caller the medical dispatcher must ensure they keep the caller calm in order to get all the information needed for an accurate response. They may also have to give advice to people facing life-threatening situations, which can be challenging. They also must help people to cope and deal with the situation in the best way possible until the ambulance arrives. Medical dispatchers with more experience may be involved in explaining complex procedures, such as delivering a baby over the telephone to a caller. A medical dispatcher should obtain some of the following skills: the ability to record and process information accurately and have good keyboard skills, they should enjoy helping people, strong sense of responsibility and a serious attitude to work, good organisation skills, stay calm under pressure, good telephone manner and good spoken communication skills and lastly have good eyesight and hearing.

Question 9

An emergency medical dispatcher always answers 999 calls from the public and GP's.

Answer [   ]

Question 10

A medical dispatcher should have good keyboard skills.

Answer [   ]

Question 11

Emergency medical dispatchers are required to pass a medical.

Answer [   ]

Question 12

When the emergency medical dispatcher answers urgent calls made to the control centre, they are working under the direction of the control officer.

Answer [   ]

VERBAL REASONING COMPREHENSION EXERCISE

Read the following passage before answering the questions as either true, false or cannot say.

The role of the Patient Transport service (PTS), also known as Ambulance care assistants is to drive service users such as elderly, disabled and vulnerable people to and from day care centres, outpatient clinics, and to routine hospital appointments. PTS drivers usually transports the same service users on a regular basis therefore will get to know some of the patients who use the service. Some patients who use the service may lead isolated lives and feel anxious about their hospital visit. Depending on the type of vehicle the Patient Transport driver will drive, they may be based at a depot at a large hospital where there are a team of other assistants. A driver will cover a certain area where they are located and will often work shifts. Lifting and moving some of the patients in and out of the vehicle are also part of their duties. It is essential that the driver ensures the patients are all comfortable and safe during the transport journey and that the patients are on time for their appointments. The Ambulance Care Assistants are also trained in resuscitation; this is in case of an emergency if any of the patients are taken ill whilst in their care. Other duties may include ensuring the vehicle is kept clean and tidy and also keeping records that are accurate as to the journeys they have undertaken. The Patient Transport Service vehicles are designed for comfort and safety of the patients. On average Patient Transport Service crews carry approximately over 1 million patients a year, which means there is over 4500 journeys a day. The members of the patient transport service team are trained as ambulance care assistants and obtain the knowledge of comprehensive first aid, driving skills and patient moving and handling skills. The role of a Patient Transport Service team member is a rewarding, challenging and demanding job role. In some areas the Patient Transport team may provide non patient transport service within the health environment for example they may transport medical samples and supplies and also transport medical staff to different locations. Due to PTS team members occasionally having to transport lab specimens, blood samples and similar items they must also be trained in transportation of bio-hazardous items. The patients that are being transported do not require the accident and emergency service, they are usually being transported because they are being transferred between hospitals, they have been dis-charged, they may have been admitted to hospital, requiring treatment or investigation at hospital or attending outpatient appointments at hospital.

Question 13

Depending on the type of vehicle the Patient Transport driver will drive they will not be based at a depot at a large hospital where there are a team of other assistants.

Answer

Question 14

The Patient Transport team may transport medical supplies if required.

Answer

Question 15

The Patient Transport service (PTS) are also known as Ambulance care operatives.

Answer

VERBAL REASONING COMPREHENSION EXERCISE

Read the following passage before answering the questions as either true, false or cannot say.

The NHS is divided into two sections, primary and secondary care. Primary care is the first point of contact for most people, this care is delivered by a wide range of independent contractors which include GP's, Dentists, pharmacists and optometrists. Parts of the primary care are also the NHS walk-in centres, opticians and the NHS direct. In charge of the primary care is The Primary Care Trusts (PCT's) they play a major part in commissioning secondary care and providing community care services. The Primary Care Trust control 80% of the NHS budget and are central to the National Health Trust. The Primary Care trust is made from local organisations, so they have an understanding of what the members of their community need therefore they can ensure the organisations providing health and social care services are working effectively. Secondary care, also known as acute healthcare can be either emergency care or elective care. Elective care is planned specialist medical care or surgery, following usually from a referral from a primary or community health care professional for example a GP. There are 12 ambulance trusts in England and the emergency vehicles are provided by the NHS ambulance services trusts. The care trusts that the NHS provide, deliver care in health and social fields. The local PCT oversee the NHS mental health services trust, which provide mental health care in England. Other agencies controlled by the NHS are the National Institute for Health and Clinical Excellence. The agencies involved in the Secondary Care are; Emergency and urgent care, ambulance trusts, NHS trusts, Mental health trusts and Care trusts. The Acute trusts within the NHS are what the hospitals are managed by. They ensure that the hospitals are providing high quality health care and ensure that they are spending their money efficiently. They also have the power to decide how a hospital will develop, so that their services improve. The Acute trusts employ a large section of the NHS workforce, such as nurses, doctors, pharmacists, midwives and health visitors. They also employ people doing jobs related to medicine and other non-medical staff. All together there are many different agencies and staff involved in the structure of the NHS and ensuring our Health care service works efficiently.

Question 16

The Primary Care Trust do not control 20% of the NHS budget.

Answer

Question 17

The NHS are responsible for spending their budget wisely.

Answer

Question 18

NHS direct forms part of primary care.

Answer

Question 19

The Acute trusts employ paramedics.

Answer

VERBAL REASONING COMPREHENSION EXERCISE

Read the following passage before answering the questions as either true, false or cannot say.

The ambulance service looks for self-motivated, enthusiastic people from different backgrounds to work as part of their team. The ambulance service encourages and values diversity within the workforce. Ensuring each individual feels comfortable, included and appreciated for their work is extremely important in the ambulance service. With training and employment opportunities it is important to provide and advertise without regard to gender, age, race, religion or belief, disability status or any other aspect that relates to an individual's personal background. The ambulance service works towards ensuring all employees are working in an environment which treats each individual with respect and that includes everyone. The working environment is also free from discrimination, harassment and there is no unequal treatment. The ambulance service thinks it is important to encourage staff from diverse backgrounds that represent the population, this helps to secure a diverse workforce. It is one of the NHS policies that no job applicant, service user or employee receives less favourable treatment on the grounds of their age, gender, disability, ethnic origin, marital status, religion or sexual orientation. Valuing individual's differences is what diversity is about. Working towards the diversity approach means that you recognise, value and manage the differences to ensure all employees are able to contribute and realise their full potential. By recognising and valuing differences this helps to make the working environment a more enjoyable place. The NHS wants to ensure that they are a fair employer achieving equality of opportunity and outcomes in the workplace. It important to embrace diversity and ensure that equality of opportunity is there for all.

Question 20

Diversity were past winners of the UK Britain's Got Talent Sow.

Answer [   ]

Question 21

There is unequal treatment in the ambulance service workplace.

Answer [   ]

Question 22

NHS policy states that no job applicant, service user or employee receives less favourable treatment on the grounds of their age.

Answer [   ]

ANSWERS TO VERBAL REASONING COMPREHENSION EXERCISES

1. False	12. True
2. Cannot say	13. False
3. Cannot say	14. True
4. True	15. False
5. False	16. True
6. False	17. Cannot say
7. False	18. True
8. Cannot say	19. Cannot say
9. False	20. Cannot say
10. True	21. False
11. Cannot say	22. True

MEMORY TEST

Some NHS trusts may require you to sit a memory test as part of their application process. You will normally receive a pamphlet or small written notebook a couple of weeks before your assessment date. You will be required to read and learn the information before you attend the assessment day. When you arrive at the assessment you will be required to recall the information and answer questions based on the content. You will not be able to refer to the information, or notes that you have made during the test. This test assesses your ability to recall information given under timed conditions.

During your paramedic training you will be required to absorb a lot of information and this test is designed to assess your memory and information recalling capability.

On the following pages I have provided you with two exercises to help you prepare for this type of test. Please note that the exercises provided are for practice purposes only and are not the exact tests you will sit on the day.

To begin with, allow yourself two minutes only to read the passage. You are not permitted to take notes. The information contained within each passage relates to the work of a paramedic and will be useful to learn as part of your preparation. Once the two minutes are up, turn over the page and answer the questions. Do not refer back to the information whilst answering the questions.

Once you have finished the first exercise, move on to the next one.

MEMORY TEST EXERCISE 1

Read the following passage for two minutes only before answering the questions on the next page.

When answering the questions you are not permitted to refer back to the passage.

The Ambulance Service has undergone a large number of significant changes. In recent years there has been an enormous investment in the training and development of ambulance crews resulting in more effective patient care than ever before.

Every single year hundreds of thousands of people in the United Kingdom will use the Ambulance Service for incidents ranging from heart attacks to broken limbs. Only 10% of the total workload of a typical Ambulance Service is made up by responding to 999 calls. The ambulance crews who make up the emergency response team will usually consist of a fully qualified paramedic and an emergency care assistant. It is their responsibility to ensure that the highest level of patient care is provided to the members of the community in which they serve.

In addition to their emergency work, the Ambulance Service is also involved with additional duties such as Patient Transport Service (PTS).

The paramedics and emergency care assistants whom form part of the ambulance crew are fully competent in their role and can deal with many different types of incidents such as cardiac arrest and road traffic collisions.

In order to carry out their role effectively they will use a wide range of comprehensive equipment such as heart defibrillators, oxygen, intravenous drips, spinal and traction splints, and a variety of drugs for medical and traumatic emergencies.

MEMORY TEST QUESTIONS FOR EXERCISE 1

Question 1

Approximately how many people use the Accident and Emergency Service every year?

Answer: _____

Question 2

In recent years there has been an enormous investment in what?

Answer: _____

Question 3

What percentage of an Ambulance Service's work is taken up by responding to 999 calls?

Answer: _____

Question 4

What does a typical ambulance emergency crew comprise of?

Answer: _____

Question 5

Name 2 different types of equipment that can be found in an ambulance.

Answer: _____

_____

MEMORY TEST ANSWERS FOR EXERCISE 1

Question 1
Hundreds of thousands of people.

Question 2
The training and development of ambulance crews.

Question 3
10%

Question 4
A paramedic and an emergency care assistant

Question 5
- Heart defibrillators;
- Oxygen;
- Intravenous drips;
- Spinal and traction splints;
- A variety of drugs for medical and traumatic emergencies.

MEMORY TEST EXERCISE 2

Read the following passage for two minutes only before answering the questions on the following page.

When answering the questions you are not permitted to refer back to the passage.

Non-Emergency Work

The Patient Transport Service (PTS) is a vital part of the Ambulance Service. In basic terms the role of the PTS is to provide transport for a variety of patients such as the following:

- Outpatients;
- Non emergency hospital transfers;
- Those non-emergency patients who cannot attend hospital via their own means;
- Routine checkups and appointments;
- Geriatric and psycho-geriatric day care patients.

PTS staff, usually under the role of ambulance care assistants, will crew a specially designed ambulance which has the ability to transport a number of patients in a safe and effective manner. At the rear of the PTS vehicle there will normally be a tail lift which will allow patients to be safely lifted onto, and off the vehicle when required. Ambulance care assistants are trained in the particular needs of their patients and they will also hold qualifications in first aid, specialist driving skills, patient moving and manual handling techniques, basic life support and patient care skills.

Whilst the role of the PTS does not involve responding to emergency incidents they are crucial to the efficient and effective running of the Ambulance Service. Without their work the Ambulance Service would not be able to operate.

In some services a number of PTS crews are specially trained as high dependency teams, which are available for patients with specific clinical needs during transport.

MEMORY TEST QUESTIONS FOR EXERCISE 2

Question 1

What does PTS stand for?

Answer: _____

Question 2

Name 2 different types of patients that the PTS transport.

Answer: _____

_____

Question 3

Who are PTS ambulances manned by?

Answer: _____

Question 4

Name two areas that ambulance care assistants are trained in.

Answer: _____

_____

Question 5

The PTS uses vehicles that are fitted with what at the rear?

Answer: _____

MEMORY TEST ANSWERS FOR EXERCISE 2

Question 1
Patient Transport Services.

Question 2
Outpatients, Non-emergency hospital transfers, those non-emergency patients who cannot attend hospital via their own means, Routine check ups and appointments, Geriatric and psycho-geriatric day care patients.

Question 3
Ambulance care assistants.

Question 4
Ambulance care assistants are trained in the particular needs of the their patients and they will also hold qualifications in first aid, specialist driving skills, patient moving and manual handling techniques, basic life support and patient care skills.

Question 5
Tail lifts.

CHAPTER 3
HIGHWAY CODE
TEST QUESTIONS

During the paramedic selection process you will have to undertake a driving test which includes a Highway Code assessment. Within this section of the guide I have provided you with a host of sample questions to help you prepare.

The only effective way to prepare for this part of the assessment is to obtain a copy of the Highway Code and learn it!

There is no time limit to the following test. Work through the 50 questions and see how many you get correct.

1. When is it acceptable to ignore a traffic light?

a. When turning left

b. When a car passenger is pregnant and in labour

c. When there are no other cars in sight

d. Never

2. When are you permitted to use the horn?

a. At all times

b. Between 5am and 2am

c. Between 7am and 11.30pm

d. From sunset to sunrise

3. What's the speed limit for cars & motorcycles in built-up areas?

a. 20mph

b. 30mph

c. 35mph

d. 40km/h

4. What's the difference between speed limits on dual carriage-ways and speed limits on motorways for cars and motorcycles?

a. 0mph

b. 10mph

c. 20mph

d. 30mph

5. What's the typical total stopping distance for a car at 40mph?

a. 36m

b. 46m

c. 56m

d. 66m

6. Which of the following is not true?

a. While driving you must not drive dangerously.

b. While driving you must not drive without care and attention

c. While driving you must not drive without style and panache

d. While driving you must not drive without consideration for other road users

7. When driving in built-up areas, which one of the following do you need to look out for?

a. Children directing traffic

b. Children emerging from driveways

c. Children driving vehicles

d. Children running out from between parked cars

8. What should you not do in a street with traffic calming measures?

a. Reduce your speed

b. Allow cyclists and motorcyclists room to pass through them

c. Avoid overtaking other moving road users while in these areas

d. Speed up in between each speed bump

9. Which of these is not necessary before moving off?

a. Use all mirrors to check the road first

b. Look around to check the blind spots

c. Sound your horn to ensure it's working

d. Signal if necessary before moving out

10. What MSM is important as you set off on a journey?

a. Make up, Sandwich, Mobile

b. Move, Speedily, Mate

c. Mirror, Signal, Manoeuvre

d. Mirror, Switch on, Move off

11. An MOT certificate is normally valid for how long?

a. three years after the date it was issued

b. 10,000 miles

c. one year after the date it was issued

d. 30,000 miles

12. How long will a Statutory Off Road Notification (SORN) last for?

a. 12 months

b. 24 months

c. 3 years

d. 10 years

13. You have just passed your practical test. You do not hold a full licence in another category. Within two years you get six penalty points on your licence. What will you have to do? (select 2 answers)

a. Retake only your theory test

b. Retake your theory and practical tests

c. Retake only your practical test

d. Reapply for your full licence immediately

e. Reapply for your provisional licence

14. When you apply to renew your Vehicle Excise Duty (tax disc) you must have:

a. the old tax disc

b. the handbook

c. a valid driving licence

d. valid insurance

15. What is the maximum specified fine for driving without insurance?

a. £50

b. £500

c. £1000

d. £5000

16. If there are no speed limit signs on the road, how is a 30 mph limit indicated?

a. By hazard warning lines

b. By street lighting

c. By pedestrian islands

d. By double or single yellow lines

17. At a pelican crossing, what does a flashing amber light mean?

a. You must not move off until the lights stop flashing

b. You must give way to pedestrians still on the crossing

c. You can move off, even if pedestrians are still on the crossing

d. You must stop because the lights are about to change to red

18. At a busy unmarked crossroads, which of the following has priority?

a. Vehicles going straight ahead

b. Vehicles turning right

c. None of the vehicles

d. The vehicles that arrived first

19. In which TWO places should you NOT park?

a. Near a school entrance

b. Near a police station

c. In a side road

d. At a bus stop

e. In a one-way street

20. You are travelling on a motorway. You MUST stop when signalled to do so by which of these?

a. Flashing amber lights above your lane

b. A Highways Agency Traffic Officer

c. Pedestrians on the hard shoulder

d. A driver who has broken down

21. Which TWO of the following are correct? When overtaking at night you should:

a. wait until a bend so that you can see the oncoming headlights

b. sound your horn twice before moving out

c. be careful because you can see less

d. beware of bends in the road ahead

e. put headlights on full beam

22. Traffic calming measures are used to

a. stop road rage

b. help overtaking

c. slow traffic down

d. help parking

23. You are towing a small trailer on a busy three-lane motorway. All the lanes are open. You must

a. not exceed 60 mph

b. not overtake

c. have a stabiliser fitted

d. use only the left and centre lanes

24. A driver does something that upsets you. You should

a. try not to react

b. let them know how you feel

c. flash your headlights several times

d. sound your horn

25. In areas where there are 'traffic calming' measures you should

a. always travel at the speed limit

b. position in the centre of the road

c. only slow down if pedestrians are near

d. travel at a reduced speed

26. A person has been injured. They may be suffering from shock. What are the warning signs to look for?

a. Flushed complexion

b. Warm dry skin

c. Slow pulse

d. Pale grey skin

27. You are approaching a roundabout. There are horses just ahead of you. You should

a. be prepared to stop

b. treat them like any other vehicle

c. give them plenty of room

d). accelerate past as quickly as possible

e. sound your horn as a warning

28. A horse rider is in the left-hand lane approaching a roundabout. You should expect the rider to

a. go in any direction

b. turn right

c. turn left

d. go ahead

29. You see a pedestrian with a dog. The dog has a yellow or burgundy coat. This especially warns you that the pedestrian is

a. elderly

b. dog training

c. colour blind

d. deaf

30. You should never wave people across at pedestrian crossings because

a) there may be another vehicle coming

b) they may not be looking

c) it is safer for you to carry on

d) they may not be ready to cross

31. A long, heavily-laden lorry is taking a long time to overtake you. What should you do?

a. Speed up

b. Slow down

c. Hold your speed

d. Change direction

32. What should you use your horn for?

a. To alert others to your presence

b. To allow you right of way

c. To greet other road users

d. To signal your annoyance

33. At a puffin crossing, which colour follows the green signal?

a. Steady red

b. Flashing amber

c. Steady amber

d. Flashing green

34. A vehicle has a flashing green beacon. What does this mean?

a. A doctor is answering an emergency call

b. The vehicle is slow-moving

c. It is a motorway police patrol vehicle

d. The vehicle is carrying hazardous chemicals

35. You should ONLY flash your headlights to other road users

a. to show that you are giving way

b. to show that you are about to turn

c. to let them know you are there

d. to tell them that you have right of way

36. The conditions are good and dry. You could use the 'two-second rule'

a. before restarting the engine after it has stalled

b. to keep a safe gap from the vehicle in front

c. before using the 'Mirror-Signal-Manoeuvre' routine

d. when emerging on wet roads

37. Your mobile phone rings while you are on the motorway. Before answering you should

a. stop in a safe place before answering it

b. answer it

c. pull up on the hard shoulder

d. quickly answer it and tell them you'll call them back later

38. A bus is stopped at a bus stop ahead of you. Its right-hand indicator is flashing. You should

a. quickly speed up to get past it

b. pretend you haven't noticed it

c. slow down and give way as soon as it is safe to do so

d. sound your horn

39. Your vehicle pulls to one side when braking. You should

a. change the tyres around

b. use your handbrake to compensate

c. consult a garage as soon as possible

d. get it checked out at the next MOT

40. In windy conditions you need to take extra care when

a. driving up hills

b. passing pedal cyclists

c. filling up with petrol

d. driving on residential roads

41. You are driving along a motorway and become tired. You should

a. pull up on the hard shoulder and rest

b. stop at the next service station and rest

c. get off at the next exit and rest

d. wind down the window and turn up your radio

42. You want to reverse into a side road. You are not sure that the area behind your car is clear. What should you do?

a. have a look through the rear window

b. look in the mirror to check for obstructions

c. reverse with your horn sounding

d. get out and check

43. To help keep your vehicle secure at night where should you park?

a. in a well-lit area

b. under a tree

c. in a quiet, secluded road

d. outside a police station

44. As a driver what does the term Blind Spot mean?

a. an area not seen in your left mirror

b. an area not seen in your right mirror

c. an area not seen when your eyes are closed

d. an area not seen in your mirrors

45. Tailgating means

a. following another vehicle too closely

b. reversing into a space

c. using the rear door of your car

d. driving through gates too fast

46. How can you tell if you are driving on ice?

a. your steering becomes heavier

b. the car makes less noise

c. the steering becomes lighter

d. the care makes more noise

47. Anti-lock brakes are of most use when you are

a. braking excessively

b. not braking at all

c. out of MOT

d. driving normally

48. A person herding sheep asks you to stop. You should

a. ignore them

b. pull over and turn off your engine

c. ignore them and sound your horn

d. carry on driving but at reduced speed

49. You are about to drive home. You cannot find the glasses you need to wear. You should

 THE **TESTING** SERIES

a. borrow a friends glasses and drive home slowly

b. only drive home when the roads are quiet

c. drive home but go through the back roads

d. find an alternative way to get home other than driving

50. Where should you take particular care to look out for motorcyclists and cyclists?

a. at junctions

b. on pavements

c. on dual-carriageways

d. at zebra crossings

ANSWERS TO HIGHWAY CODE TEST QUESTIONS

1. d	26. d
2. c	27. a and c
3. b	28. a
4. a	29. d
5. a	30. a
6. c	31. b
7. d	32. a
8. d	33. c
9. c	34. a
10. c	35. c
11. c	36. b
12. a	37. a
13. b and e	38. c
14. d	39. c
15. d	40. b
16. b	41. c
17. b	42. d
18. c	43. a
19. a and d	44. d
20. b	45. a
21. c and d	46. c
22. c	47. a
23. a and d	48. b
24. a	49. d
25. d	50. a

A FEW FINAL WORDS

You have now reached the end of the guide and will no doubt be far better prepared for the paramedic/emergency care assistant selection process. Just before you go, consider the following.

The majority of candidates who pass the paramedic selection process have a number of common attributes. These are as follows:

1. They believe in themselves.

The first factor is self-belief. Regardless of what anyone tells you, you can become a paramedic. Just like any job of this nature, you have to be prepared to work hard in order to be successful. Make sure you have the self-belief to pass the selection process and fill your mind with positive thoughts.

2. They prepare fully.

The second factor is preparation. Those people who achieve in life prepare fully for every eventuality and that is what you must do when you apply to become a paramedic. Work very hard and especially concentrate on your weak areas.

3. They persevere.

Perseverance is a fantastic word. Everybody comes across obstacles or setbacks in their life, but it is what you do about those setbacks that is important. If you fail at something, then ask yourself 'why' you have failed. This will allow you to improve for next time and if you keep improving and trying, success will eventually follow. Apply this same method of thinking when you apply to become a paramedic.

4. They are self-motivated.

How much do you want this job? Do you want it, or do you really want it?

When you apply to join the Ambulance Service you should want it more than anything in the world. Your levels of self-motivation will shine through on your application and during your interview. For the weeks and months leading up to the paramedic selection process, be motivated as best you can and always keep your fitness levels up as this will serve to increase your levels of motivation.

Work hard, stay focused and be what you want…

Richard McMunn

Richard McMunn

Visit www.how2become.co.uk to find more titles and courses that will help you to pass the paramedic selection process:

- 1 Day intensive paramedic training courses

- Paramedic interview DVD's and books

- Online paramedic tests

- Psychometric testing books and CDs

WWW.HOW2BECOME.CO.UK